# THE
# INDY CAR RACING
# HANDBOOK

**Thumbs up for Fittipaldi**: But it was not to be when, at the penultimate race of the 1993 Indy car racing season, the former two-time World Champion fell two points short of staying in contention as the only remaining challenger to Mansell's unique record of holding both the Indy and F-1 crowns simultaneously.

**COVER PICTURE:** After setting the fastest time in the opening practice session, Mansell loses control entering Turn One, Phoenix, at 180 mph and slides sideways before backing into (and punching a hole through) the concrete retaining wall surrounding the one mile oval. Knocked unconscious, Nigel was flown by helicopter to Good Samaritan Hospital where he was found to have suffered a mild concussion but no other serious injuries. "The back end went away and I said to myself 'No way; there's no way I can get it back' ". Mansell later recalled. "So I ducked down. The next thing I remember is waking up in the helicopter. It must have been a long time because the helicopter was landing."

# THE
# INDY CAR RACING
# HANDBOOK

## DAVID PHILLIPS
With photographs by
## ART FLORES

Foreword by
## MARIO ANDRETTI

SIDGWICK & JACKSON
LONDON

*"To my long-suffering wife Mary who has spent far too many weekends as a single parent."*

A Cooling Brown Production for Sidgwick and Jackson

*Editor* James Harrison
*Sub Editor* Ann Kay
*Art Director* Sue Rawkins
*Designer* Malcolm Smythe
*Picture Researcher* Phil O'Connor
*Page make-up and track designs* Mick Goodrum
*Charts and tables* Jo Cooling

Cooling Brown
9-11 High Street,
Hampton-upon Thames,
Middlesex TW12 2SA

First published 1993 by Sidgwick & Jackson Limited
a division of Pan Macmillan Publishers Limited
Cavaye Place, London SW10 9PG
and Basingstoke

Associated companies throughout the world

ISBN 0-283-06203-7

Copyright © 1993 Cooling Brown

A CIP catalogue record for this book is available from the British Library.

Printed in the UK

# CONTENTS

"1993 was a remarkable year for Indy car racing. Of course, any time someone with the status of Nigel Mansell comes into a racing series it's a win-win situation for everyone involved.

The presence of the reigning World Champion heightens international awareness of Indy car racing and brings added value to the PPG Indy Car World Series for our sponsors and fans, and guarantees a big boost in television ratings. At the same time, people around the world have been exposed to a form of racing which I believe is second to none in the challenge it presents to drivers and teams, and the excitement it offers the fans.

I've had the good fortune to compete in just about every form of motor racing during my career, from Formula One to Indy cars; from stock cars to midgets; from the Can-Am to the Pikes Peak Hillclimb. And while my sense of satisfaction has always been based on the results, no matter who, what or where I raced, looking back I have to say that 1969 was probably the most satisfying season of my career.

That season I won races on road courses, superspeedways (the picture above shows me after my Indianapolis 500 victory that year), short ovals, dirt tracks and at Pikes Peak – all counting for the national championship. No matter where we went, I won. Believe me, that meant a lot to me then, and it means maybe even more to me now.

While we no longer race at Pikes Peak or on the dirt tracks, the PPG Indy Car World Series

remains the most demanding test of a driver's versatility, more so even than Formula One. No other major series races on permanent road courses, short ovals, superspeedways and street circuits. It's a helluva' mix and, from a driver's stand point, you have to be strong everywhere to be a factor in the championship.

Indy car racing also has a lot to offer the fans. The 1993 championship went down to the final two races, just as it has every year since 1982. The restrictive rules, the different kinds of tracks and the closeness of the competition make for unpredictable results. In the early days of CART, if you were with a top flight team you were pretty much assured of a top five finish any time your equipment lasted to the chequered flag. Not any more. It's just amazing how hard you have to drive to break into the top five. That kind of competition is a strong attraction to fans, sponsors, teams, manufacturers and drivers – all of whom are being attracted to Indy car racing in increasing numbers.

I hope you've had the chance to watch some Indy car racing this summer and that, with the help of *THE INDY CAR RACING HANDBOOK* you'll enjoy the 1994 PPG Indy Car World Series even more."

"... the PPG Indy Car World Series remains the most demanding test of a driver's versatility, more so even than Formula One."

# THE WORD IS OUT

Anyone with even a passing interest in motorsports has heard of the Indianapolis 500 – whether they hail from Speedway, Indiana, or the Isle of Skye. But until comparatively recently, only a hard-core racing aficionado could have told you what the drivers, cars and teams that spend the month of May at the Indianapolis Motor Speedway do during the other 11 months of the year.

What they do is compete in the PPG Indy Car World Series, a series of races stretching from Surfers Paradise, Australia to Loudon, New Hampshire in the world's most versatile race cars. And from November through to February, when they're not actually racing, Indy car drivers are preparing for the forthcoming season – testing new equipment, pursuing elusive sponsorship and fulfilling commitments to existing sponsors.

The diversity of the track types – road courses, high-banked superspeedways, temporary street circuits and mile ovals – makes the PPG Indy Car World Series the world's most demanding test of a driver's versatility. Road racing specialists might win their share on the temporary circuits and road courses; the "oval-meisters" might shine on the speedways and the miles; but only a driver proficient on both road and oval tracks can win the overall PPG title.

## INDY IMPROVED

Four main factors mean that Indy car racing is no longer motorsport's best-kept secret:

◆ Since 1978 a relatively new organization called Championship Auto Racing Teams (CART) has been aggressively promoting Indy cars and developing Indy's own distinct identity (see also History in the making).

◆ In 1979, PPG Industries, the world's largest producer of automotive and industrial coatings, came on board as the title sponsor of CART's new Indy car series.

◆ CART added more permanent road courses such Laguna Seca, Road America and Mid-Ohio, and later temporary circuits (à la Monaco Grand Prix ) in the streets of cities from Long Beach to Toronto.

◆ International drivers have consistently shown that they find the PPG Series an increasingly viable alternative to Formula One – from early '80s trailblazers such as Italy's Teo Fabi and ireland's Derek Daly to Brazil's Emerson Fittipaldi, culminating in Nigel Mansell's much-publicized conversion to Indy car in 1993.

*Rookies race it out: Stefan Johansson and Robby Gordon, both rookies at Phoenix, do battle during the Valvoline 200. Johansson was an early retirement while Gordon charged from 20th to third before crashing.*

# BEHIND THE SCENES — TURBULENT TRAILS

There are now 16 races that make up the PPG Indy Car World Series: that much is simple fact. After that it can get somewhat confusing. Of the 16 races, 15 are CART-sanctioned, but one – the Indianapolis 500 – is sanctioned by another organization called the United States Auto Club (USAC, see *US Motorsports Family Tree, page 124*). Despite this split-sanctioning, winning race points at the Indianapolis 500 definitely counts towards the PPG Series title. This was not always so.

## RIVALRY . . .

In 1979, a breakaway group of Indy car team owners, dissatisfied with USAC's administration, formed CART and inaugurated their own racing series. In those turbulent times, drivers, owners, promoters and sponsors chose to side either with CART or, particularly in the case of the Indianapolis Motor Speedway, with USAC. As the PPG

Series gained ascendancy, most tracks switched to CART. Indianapolis did not. In fact, the '81 and '82 Indianapolis 500s did not count towards the PPG championship. That changed in 1983, when PPG announced a $165,000 prize fund for the 33 qualifiers for the race.

CART initially had a board of directors made up of team owners, chairman, and representatives from the drivers and mechanics. To create stability and profitability for the team owners, CART established a system in which team owners who entered cars in all or most of the races were eligible to purchase one of 24 CART franchises. The distribution of prize money was subsequently weighted in favour of franchise holders. The franchises are reviewed at the end of each season and teams that did not enter all the races may be asked to sell their franchises to non-franchise teams with a better attendance record.

## . . . AND RECONCILIATION?

In 1989, the team owners created a new board consisting of all the franchise holders. By 1993, the unwieldy 24-vote board had been replaced by one consisting of five team owners – Roger Penske, Carl Haas, Dale Coyne, Derrick Walker and Jim Hall, with the CART chairman Bill Stokken and International Motor Speedway president Tony George as non-voting members. The reconstituted board represented a tangible step towards reconciliation between CART and the IMS, which had long been at odds over every aspect of the sport. The 1993 season saw CART and USAC agree on a common chassis rules package that will take the sport well into the latter half of the 1990s. The two remain divided on engine policies, however: USAC and Indianapolis now welcome participation by new engine suppliers, while CART's rules are far more restrictive.

9

*Sporting gestures: A product of the southern California dirt tracks, Parnelli Jones drove for JC Agajanian at various stages of his career and won a controversial Indy 500 in 1963. Many thought Jones should have been black flagged for losing oil, including Eddie Sachs who punched Jones at the victory banquet.*

# NOW THAT'S COMPETITON!

Competition is what Indy car racing is all about. The organizers' rules virtually guarantee that no single chassis or engine can dominate the sport. With all due apologies to Thomas Jefferson, when all chassis and engines are created equal it puts the racing where it belongs – in the hands of the drivers. In 1992, no fewer than 14 drivers scored top-three finishes, while six different drivers won races and seven started from pole. Perhaps the most amazing statistic of all, however, is that at Road America – a four mile, 14 turn road course – officials had to take the qualifying times to the ten thousandth of a second to determine that Paul Tracy had beaten Emerson Fittipaldi for the pole.

A major difference between Indy car and F-1 rules is in their overall philosophy, and this difference gives Indy car's competitive spirit a real boost. While Formula One embodies the leading edge of automotive technology, Indy car officials have fashioned a compromise. This compromise enables Indy cars to be technologically relevant, while also keeping a close reign on advanced, expensive technologies that do little to enhance on-track competition. So, sophisticated technologies such as computer controlled "active" suspensions, semi-automatic transmissions (in F-1, "mapping" of shift points now all but eliminates the need for a driver to change gears himself), and traction control (which cuts out wheel spin when an excessive amount of throttle is applied) are **not** permitted in Indy car racing.

*Caution: Objects in mirror are closer than they appear:*
*Emerson Fittipaldi heads a tight pack of competitors at Long Beach. The Brazilian however failed by one place to be in the final points-getters for this race. Close competition is the essence of Indy car racing.*

The Lola T9300 Ford/Cosworth XB that Nigel Mansell first drove in January 1993, and the Williams FW14B Renault that he drove to nine victories in 1992, appear quite similar. Underneath the fibreglass and carbon fibre, however, the contemporary Indy car is a very different piece of machinery from its F-1 counterpart.

## CHASSIS STYLE

For example, CART rules state that Indy cars must weigh a minimum of 703kg with coolants and lubricants. In contrast, the Formula One minimum weight is 500kg. Formula One and CART also take very different approaches to "ground effects" technology, which makes use of curved underbodies to turn a racing car into an inverted airplane wing – creating downforce rather than lift. While Formula One "flat bottom" regulations prohibit curved underbody and sidepod bellies, Indy car rules allow for "limited" ground effects. Curved underbodies are permitted but the sliding skirts once used to contain the "spillage" of air from the sides of the car are prohibited.

## ENGINE RULES

Of course, it's not just the chassis and suspension components that have to stand up to 500 miles of competition at 225 mph. The same basic engine has to be equally capable of pulling an Indy car from 25 mph up to 175 mph on Long Beach's Shoreline Straight and running wide open at 225 mph for long stretches at Indianapolis and Michigan. The engine must cope with the fact that

its only respite comes during pit stops to refuel and change tyres, or caution periods in the event of an accident.

Three engine types are permitted in Indy car racing:
◆ turbocharged, four cycle, overhead camshaft engines with a maximum displacement of 2.65 litres;
◆ production-derived, single, non-overhead camshaft engines with push rod operated valves and a maximum displacement of 3.43 litres;
◆ since 1991, USAC has also recognized naturally aspirated, domestically produced six litre V-8s; however, none have yet entered the Indy 500.

**Is it an Indy or F-1 car?:** *Exterior dimensions are similar – the wheelbase, front and rear tracks of the '93 Indy cars are within a few centimetres of their F-1 counterparts – but there are significant differences in aerodynamics, weight, gearbox, fuel – not to mention performance and sponsors' logos!*

CART and USAC differ on their turbocharging rules. CART permits manifold pressure of 45in of mercury on full race engines and, in 1991, raised the allowable boost for stock blocks from 45in to 50in. USAC, on the other hand, has long given stock blocks a significant advantage, allowing them up to 55in of boost while retaining the 45in maximum on race engines. Although the stock blocks remained uncompetitive in CART races with 50in of boost, with 55in they were a real force at Indianapolis in years gone by, particularly in qualifying. Roberto Guerrero won the pole for the 1992 Indianapolis 500 at a speed of 232.482 mph with a stock block Buick, for

example. However, reliability proved to be the stock block's Achilles heel and Al Unser's third place in the 1992 Indy 500 has been the Buick's high water mark.

In most respects, Formula One engine regulations are less complex and more open than the rules of CART or USAC:
◆ Indy car engines are limited to a maximum of eight cylinders, but F-1 engines can have as many as twelve;
◆ Indy car rules dictate maximum displacement based on engine type, whereas F-1 has just one rule: a maximum displacement of 3.5 litres.

But despite differences, most Indy car engines provide roughly 750-780 bhp (break horse power) – about the same as a good F-1 engine.

## FUEL RULES

Indy cars run on methanol fuel, which is less volatile than the gasoline used in F-1 and is, therefore, less likely to ignite in the refuelling process during the critical pit stops. Indy cars are required to average 1.8 miles per gallon of methanol during a race.

To ensure that they do, CART only issues enough fuel at the beginning of the race for a car to complete a handful of warm-up and pace laps (Indy cars use rolling starts rather than the standing starts preferred in Europe) and run the race distance while burning no more than 1.8 miles per gallon. In F-1, cars run flag-to-flag without refuelling, (though tyre stops are not unusual). F-1 also allows any number of people to work on a car during pit stops, while CART and USAC limit the number to six – one for each tyre plus one to refuel and another to hold the fuel vent.

# INDY CAR — INSIDE OUT

## LOLA CHASSIS/CHEVROLET INDY V8-C ENGINE

### CAR/CHASSIS SPEC

| | |
|---|---|
| Type | Lola T9300 |
| Weight | 1,550 pounds (excludes driver and fuel) |
| Weight distribution | Front/Rear – 45%/55% |
| Track | Front/Rear – 78$^1/_2$/80$^1/_2$ inches |
| Wheelbase | 111 inches |
| Length | 15ft. 5 in. (185 in) |
| Fuel capacity | 40 gallons |
| Steering | Rack and Pinion |
| Front Suspension | Push Rod, Upper Rocker, Inboard Springs and Dampers |
| Rear Suspension | Push Rod, Upper Rocker, Inboard Springs and Dampers |
| Wheels | Magnesium (Mfg: Dymag) |
| | Height: 16 inches (Front and Rear) |
| | Width: *Front* 10$^3/_4$ inches, *Rear* 15 inches |
| Tyres | Goodyear Racing Eagle Radials |
| | *Front* Height 16 inches; Tread 10$^3/_4$ inches |
| | *Rear* Height 27 inches; Tread 14 inches |
| Brakes | ALCON |
| Paint | PPG |

## ENGINE SPEC

| | |
|---|---|
| Engine | Chevrolet Indy V8-C |
| Type | 90 degree V–8; Aluminium Block & Heads |
| Bore x Stroke | 88.0mm x 54.4mm |
| Displacement | 2647cc (161.5 cubic in) |
| Compression ratio | 11.0 : 1 |
| Fuel System | Ilmor Electronic Fuel Injection |
| Valve Gear | Gear-driven, Overhead Cams, Four Valves per Cylinder |
| Horsepower | 700–plus at 12,000 RPM |
| Weight | 325 pounds |
| Manufacturer | Ilmor Engines |
| Rebuilds | VDS Engines |
| Fuel | Methanol |
| Oil | Valvoline High Performance Synthetic Racing Motor Oil/20W50 |
| Onboard Computers | Pi Electronics |

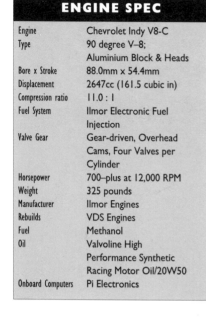

## RATING AN INDY CAR PERFORMANCE

Given their significant edge in lightness and advanced technology, as well as a slightly larger tyre "footprint", it should come as no surprise that F-1 cars are faster than Indy cars on comparable road circuits. A comparison of lap times at the old Detroit street circuit confirms this: the 1989 Indy car pole time was more than a second slower than the Formula One pole time of 1988, despite the fact that a chicane used during the F-1 races had been eliminated for the Indy car race.

But while their robust minimum weight makes Indy cars comparatively ungainly on road and street circuits such as Detroit, that extra 200kg is absolutely essential when the Indy cars race at speedways such as Indianapolis and Michigan, where average lap speeds of 225 are common, and where the consequences of a mechanical failure or driver error are instantaneous and severe. The AVERAGE speed at Indy or Michigan is 25 mph higher than the top speed at Silverstone; cars enter Turn One at Indianapolis travelling in excess of 230 mph and the edge of the track is marked not by a soft gravel pit but a stout concrete wall.

Put simply, an Indy car has to be heavier and more durable than an F-1 car in order to make racing at the speedways and mile ovals safe. And recent Indy car history has often seen significant changes in chassis construction rules, aimed at improving driver safety.

## LOLA – ANOTHER BRITISH SUCCESS

Lola Cars Ltd, of Huntingdon, Cambridgeshire, England, is one of the world's most successful producers of race car chassis. Founded by Eric Broadley in the early 1960s, Lola has experienced success in virtually all forms of formula and sports car racing. Since 1988, the company has been the leading manufacturer of Indy cars. Lola cars, which are imported to the United States by Carl Haas, have won the 1987, 1990, 1991, 1992 and 1993 PPG Indy car championships.

## VERY VERSATILE MODEL

The versatility of the modern Indy car is its greatest asset. In 1992, Scott Goodyear won the Michigan 500 at an average speed of 177.625 mph in essentially the same car – a Lola T9200-Chevrolet – in which Bobby Rahal won in Detroit at an average speed of 81.988 mph! Race distances vary as much as the courses and speeds. While Rahal's car covered 162 miles at Detroit, Goodyear's Lola-Chevy ran all of 500 miles at Michigan. By contrast, the 1992 F-1 calendar featured races varying in length from 161 to 193 miles at Monaco and Suzuka, respectively.

## PIT STOPS AND SLOW-DOWNS

Pit stops are among the most fascinating and exciting moments of an Indy car race. Races are literally won or lost in the pits. With cars covering the length of a football field in less than a second, a jammed wheel nut or a stubborn fuel coupling can cost drivers more time on the race track than they can ever recover.

Fuel and pit stop strategy adds a dimension to Indy car racing that F-1 only hints at with its tyre stops. Unlike Formula One, Indy car races are frequently slowed to a snail's pace for three main reasons:

◆ for "full course yellows" (when a "pace car" is dispatched to lead the field around at a moderate speed while safety workers prepare the track for a return to competition);
◆ during caution periods to facilitate clean-up and removal of damaged cars from an accident;
◆ if a driver suffers a mechanical failure and is unable to drive his car to a safe spot on the race track.

## RUNNING ON EMPTY...

Obviously, a driver who pits and takes on fuel and tyres while the rest of the field follows the pace car around at 60 or 70 mph will benefit when his competitors make their pit stops after the race has resumed. On the other hand, all but the 500-mile races are generally run with two planned pit stops – at one-third and two-thirds distance.

So, if the caution occurs at the wrong time, say at half distance, a driver who already pitted at one-third distance will not be able to take on enough fuel to make it to the finish without a third stop. However, he can make the stop at half distance and drive at a slowish pace the rest of the way, hoping to conserve enough fuel to make it to the finish. He may stop at half distance and gamble that there will be another full course yellow that will enable him to pit again while the pace is slowed; or he can elect not to pit

## MPH vs SECONDS

The clash of cultures in Indy car racing, where America's oval track and road racing heritage meet head-on 16 times a season, is nowhere more evident than during practice and qualifying. At speedways such as Indianapolis and Michigan, laps are traditionally recorded at average speeds. Thus the talk at Indianapolis in May isn't about laps of 40.8 or 39.8 seconds, but laps of 220.5 or 226.1 mph. Conversely, laps on road circuits are recorded in terms of elapsed time. So at Long Beach the talk isn't about laps at 106.5 or 104.6 mph, but laps at 53.7 or 54.7 seconds. It would then seem to follow that after a month of lap speeds (rather than times) at Indianapolis, there'd be another weekend of lap times at the Milwaukee oval. Wrong. Contrary to what you might expect, the mile ovals are gauged in terms of time. And over the winter, the word trickles out not that Nigel Mansell ran a lap at 167.4 at Phoenix, but that he turned a 21.5.

*Work that one out.*

and gamble that there WON'T be another yellow.

Although the driver makes the ultimate decision, this three-dimensional chess game is best left in the hands of the team managers, who have scores of computers at their disposal calculating the rate of fuel usage with each passing lap.

Ethereal as the pit stop strategy may be, it can also translate into fierce competition and excitement on the track. Take the 1991 Nazareth race, for example. Michael Andretti and Bobby Rahal battled for the lead through three pit stops and 194 laps, only to see Arie Luyendyk whisk from fourth place to the win in the final four laps – after making just two stops and conserving fuel in the latter stages of the race.

## FLAG SIGNALS

There are eight differently designed/coloured flags used by track-side officials to warn drivers of the following:

| | |
|---|---|
| ✗ green | start |
| ✗ yellow | caution: slow and hold position |
| ✗ yellow with 2 red vertical stripes | oil on track |
| ✗ blue with yellow diagonal stripe | another competitor is following closely |
| ✗ black | pull into pits for consultation |
| ✗ red | stop |
| ✗ white | entering last lap |
| ✗ chequered | the race is finished |

# THE QUEST FOR SAFETY

The very concept of driving around a race track at an average speed of 225 mph would seem to be diametrically opposed to the concept of safety. Nothing could be further from the truth. Both CART and USAC work tirelessly in the search for improvements in track, car and driver equipment safety.

The Indy car Safety Team is perhaps the single finest example of Indy car racing's relentless quest for safety. Founded in 1985 by Carl Horton, a leading manufacturer of emergency and rescue vehicles, the Indy car Safety Team provides state-of-the art services to the PPG Indy Car World Series through its staff of over 20 professionals and six specially equipped vehicles. The team uses two rapid response trucks, built exclusively to meet the unique demands of Indy car racing. The units are staffed by medical and emergency professionals, fitted out with fire fighting, rescue, emergency extrication and medical equipment, and

## SAFETY TEAM ON THE MOVE

Facilities provided by the Safety Team's mobile trauma unit include:

◆ oxygen;
◆ heart monitor and defibrillator;
◆ high-frequency ventilator;
◆ orthopaedic and X-ray facilities;
◆ pharmacy table;
◆ sophisticated patient monitoring system;
◆ instant computer access to medical records of all Indy drivers;
◆ separate "waiting room" for families and team members.

are positioned at each event in order to respond immediately to any incident.

The Safety Team's mobile trauma unit, stationed in the paddock, is a 40-foot, $750,000 specially-customized coach equipped with a full complement of medical trauma facilities equal to those of a small hospital (see box, "Safety Team on the Move"). Completing the fleet of safety vehicles is the unique MR-10, a fully-equipped miniature trauma and rescue cart, designed to serve limited access areas such as the pit lane and the paddock.

And beyond the race track, the Indy car Safety Team's medical staff includes world-renowned orthopaedic and critical care specialists with cutting-edge knowledge of trauma treatment, sports medicine and orthopaedic surgery.

*Blowing it:* Youthful enthusiasm overcame Canadian Paul Tracy at Phoenix. With a two-lap lead on the field, Tracy crashed trying to put another lap on third place Jimmy Vasser.

*Follow the three-million brick road:* The starting field at the 1937 Indianapolis 500 – the year when the roughest sections were resurfaced with asphalt. The track's surface (lined with 3.2 million bricks) gave it its nickname of "the brickyard".

16

## A LEGACY OF DIVERSITY

Today's PPG Indy Car World Series is recognized the world over for its remarkable diversity. Starting grids are peopled by drivers hailing from North and South America, Europe and Asia, with backgrounds ranging from Formula One to sprint cars, midgets and off-road racing. Only those drivers, teams and machines that perform equally well on super speedways, street circuits, mile ovals, permanent road courses and even an airport-turned-race-track can hope to win the PPG Championship.

This diversity is very much in keeping with a sport whose legacy includes no less than four sanctioning bodies, and a history of racing everywhere from the dusty roads of Pikes Peak to the bricks of Indianapolis, the wooden board tracks of the 1920s and the dirt tracks of the '30s, '40s, '50s and '60s; there's even a lusty controversy over who actually won the 1920 championship.

## 1900s: ON THE BOARDS

Although the first recorded American automobile race took place in 1895, the American Automobile Association (AAA) did not begin sanctioning events until 1904, when the first Vanderbilt Cup was held on the open roads of Long Island, New York. The AAA and the rival Automobile Club of America sanctioned road races throughout 1916, by which time racing on purpose-built tracks had begun to flourish.

The first of these tracks was the Indianapolis Motor Speedway, which opened in 1909 boasting a surface of crushed gravel and was repaved with bricks by the time the

inaugural Indianapolis 500 was held in 1911. But bricks weren't the only means of paving a race track. In the next few years scores of "board" tracks – paved with wooden planks – opened around the country. With smooth surfaces and steeply banked turns, these wooden tracks of a mile or more in length enabled cars to lap at speeds in excess of 140 mph during the 1920s.

Early American race cars like the 1911 Indy 500-winning Marmon Wasp had been little more than stripped-down production models, with steel ladder frames and low-revving engines displacing between 400 and 600 cubic inches and producing perhaps 100 horsepower.

In 1913, however, Frenchman Jules Goux won the Indianapolis 500 in a Peugeot which featured a 7.3 litre in-line, four-cylinder engine with dual overhead camshafts and four valves per cylinder that produced more than 160 horsepower.

Even after a 300 cubic inch displacement rule was instituted for the 1915 Indianapolis race, sophisticated European cars such as Peugeot and Mercedes continued to dominate against opposition from American cars produced by Stutz, Duesenberg, Miller and Frontenac.

Many historians date the nucleus of the AAA's national championship to 1916, a season that featured nine board track races, two road races (one each on concrete and dirt) and, in the last time two events were held at Indianapolis, two on brick. The championship went to Englishman Dario Resta, who won the Indianapolis 500 and four other events in a Peugeot.

## THE '20s: INDY CAR'S GOLDEN AGE

In the wake of World War I, auto racing took hold in America. Although historians still argue over whether Gaston Chevrolet or Tommy Milton won the 1920 national championship (owing to the AAA having two different official listings for that season), there is no doubting that the "Roaring Twenties" was a golden age of American racing. The national championship consisted of as many as 26 events in a season, as racing flourished from the board tracks of Miami, Florida to Culver City, California, with the big race on the bricks of Indianapolis in between.

Although the AAA Contest Board adopted the same 3 litre maximum engine displacement rule then used by Grand Prix racing, American cars from Frontenac and, more importantly, Miller and Duesenberg, quickly gained ascendancy at Indianapolis and on the board tracks in the rest of the AAA series.

The Duesenbergs and Millers represented two different approaches to race cars. The Duesenbergs, designed and built by Fred and August Duesenberg, were noted for lightweight chassis featuring aluminum frames, while Harry Miller's cars were stronger, more durable and made use of the latest in fabrication and machining. Supercharged engines also became the rage in the 1920s, as engine builders strove to maximize power output under the three-litre and later two-litre, engine formulas.

The Duesenbergs and Millers pretty much split the winnings equally in the early half of the decade, with Jimmy Murphy also driving a "Duesie" to victory in the 1921 French Grand Prix – the last American-built car to win a Grand Prix until Dan Gurney's Eagle won in Belgium in 1967. Later on, the Millers became the cars to beat and won four straight national titles between 1926 and 1929 in the hands of men like Louis Meyer and Peter DePaolo. Another Miller driver, Frank Lockhart, seemed destined for greatness after winning the Indianapolis 500 and eight other races in 1926 and '27, but he was killed while attempting to set a land speed record in early 1928.

## THE '30s: DEPRESSION, DIRT AND JUNK

The onset of the Great Depression in 1929 led to the demise of the costly board tracks in favour of dirt tracks, and this slowed the advance of auto racing technology in the United States. Even before the world economy plunged into ruin, the AAA had been concerned about the skyrocketing costs of

17

*The rapid advance of technology saw American motorsports move from what were essentially stripped-down passenger cars in the days of the 1911 inaugural Indy 500-winning Marmon Wasp (below), to the sophisticated elegance of Harry Miller's hand built race cars (above) in little more than a decade.*

supercharging and front wheel drive. Thus in 1929 a new set of rules was introduced to enable low-cost, production-based vehicles to compete with all-out racing equipment in an effort to limit costs.

The new formula, known in some circles as the "junk formula", mandated a minimum weight of 1750 pounds, maximum engine displacement of 366 cubic inches and outlawed superchargers on four cycle engines. It also required two-seater cars. The formula attracted the attention of American automakers such as Studebaker, Stutz, Ford, Hudson and Hupmobile, who entered fleets of production-based cars in the Indianapolis 500. And while many low-budget teams were able to go racing with what amounted to stripped-down production cars fitted with

*Shaw winner: Wilbur Shaw proudly shows off his 1940 Maserati 8CTF (above). He drove to his third (and second) Indianapolis 500 win in this car.*

*"Super Tex" AJ Foyt (below) scored the first of four Indianapolis 500 wins in 1961 after a sensational duel with popular Eddie Sachs. Swapping the lead back and forth with Sachs for over 200 miles, Foyt had to stop for fuel with 15 laps to go and seemingly had no chance of winning. But Sachs stopped to change a worn right front tyre with four laps to go and Foyt's Bowes Seal Fast Special went on to victory.*

streamlined bodies, the junk formula also spawned numerous small volume custom shops making purpose-built racers for the new rules.

It was the custom-built cars from the shops of men such as "Curly" Wetteroth and Myron Stevens that did the balance of the winning in the early '30s, together with the odd Duesenberg or Miller converted to two-seater form. Concentrating almost exclusively on Indianapolis, the factory teams achieved a fair degree of success, with

Studebaker's third place in the 1932 race the high water mark; the nadir was Ford's magnificent failure in 1935 – when all five factory-entered cars dropped out with steering gear failure.

In the latter half of the decade, the rules were again brought into line with the Grand Prix rules of the time in the hopes of attracting the fabulously successful Mercedes and Auto Union factory teams to race in America. Although the Europeans did come – and win – a revitalized Vanderbilt Cup in 1936 and '37,

they never came to Indianapolis in force. But the rules enabled wealthy Americans to buy Grand Prix cars and race them in the US. Thus Wilbur Shaw won the Indianapolis 500 in 1939 and 1940 in a Maserati 8CTF. Coupled with his 1937 victory in an Offenhauser-powered Stevens chassis, Shaw joined Louis Meyer as a three-time Indy 500 winner.

### THE '40s: NOVIS AND BLUE CROWNS

While the Indianapolis 500 continued to be one of the major sports events of the year, the competition declined to as few as one other race (in 1938), and in the latter half of the 1930s the national championship consisted of, on average, a paltry three events. Even that level of competition fell away during 1942-45, when the national championship series halted in deference to the war effort, and it wasn't until 1946 that auto racing reappeared. The Indianapolis Motor Speedway, once the jewel of American racing facilities, had fallen into disrepair and only a desperate bid to save the facility by Wilbur Shaw and Indianapolis businessman Tony Hulman saved "the Brickyard" from land developers.

In order to attract as many entries as possible, the AAA-adopted rules remained similar to the pre-War era for a period but, apart from Indianapolis, the national championship was contested entirely on dirt tracks. And as prosperity returned, teams began building two types of cars for the championship – one for the dirt tracks and another, specialized car for Indianapolis.

Although it never won a championship race, one of the most legendary cars in the history of Indy car racing appeared in the late 1940s in the form of the Novi. Based on the Novi V-8 engine which first raced in 1941, the 1946 Novi was a

sleek, front wheel drive machine boasting a full length aluminum body, torsion bar suspension, an 85-gallon fuel tank – and a race weight of 1,920 pounds. Gorgeous to behold and truly terrifying to hear, the Novi topped 170 mph on the straights, set the fastest qualifying time in 1946 and '48, and won the pole in 1949 and '51. Owing to its enormous fuel consumption and tyre wear, however, a Novi never won the Memorial Day classic.

The big winners of the time were the equally beautiful Blue Crown Specials which, like the Novis, had an extremely low frontal area due to front wheel drive, but were also lightweight (1,650 pounds) and fuel efficient, typically carrying only 30 to 40 gallons of fuel. While the Novis had to make frequent stops for tyres and fuel, the Offenhauser-powered Blue Crown cars stopped just once in a 500-mile race and so won '47, '48 and '49 Indy 500s.

## THE '50s: ENTER THE "ROADSTER" . . .

In 1952 the first "roadster" was built for the Indy 500, a low-slung creation with a wide chassis that enabled the drive line to pass beside – rather than underneath – the driver, who sat on the right side of the car. In addition, the engine was tilted to the right and the resulting lower centre of gravity, combined with the favourable weight distribution stemming from the drive line and fuel tank placement, meant a roadster could corner 10-15 mph quicker than other cars of the day.

Bill "the Mad Russian" Vukovich led the 1952 Indy 500 handily in the Kurtis roadster, but crashed in the final laps when a steering arm broke. The establishment had seen the light of day, however, and the roadster design dominated the Indy 500 throughout the 1950s in the hands of men like Vukovich, Pat Flaherty, and the cigar-chewing Jimmy Bryan.

## . . . BUT SPRINTS DOMINATE DIRT TRACK

The 1950s also saw Hulman develop the Indianapolis Motor Speedway into one of the world's great sports arenas, while competition continued to flourish on scores of dirt tracks around the country and on the Pikes Peak hillclimb, a timed event on the dirt road to the 14,110 foot high crest of the Colorado landmark. While the roadster ruled at Indy, the dirt track races were still the domain of the upright sprint type cars that were little changed from pre-War days. The ubiquitous Offenhauser was an inline four-cylinder engine designed in the early '30s and developed in the 1940s and '50s by Louis Meyer and Dale Drake. It reigned supreme both at Indianapolis and on the dirt tracks in the hands of three-time national champions Bryan, Tony Bettenhausen (winner of the 1951 and '58 national championships), Chuck Stevenson, Sam Hanks, Bob Sweikert and Rodger Ward.

*"Black Jack"* Brabham caused quite a stir when he entered a car based on his World-Championship-winning Cooper Climax to Indianapolis in 1961 (right). Although overmatched in horsepower, the nimble Cooper cornered faster than the behemoths of the day and finished in a surprising ninth place.

### Indy car heroes: Al Unser

The quiet man of Indy car racing, Al Unser has let his driving do his talking since he first took up racing in 1957 at the Speedway Park in Albuquerque, New Mexico. And his driving has done a lot of talking. The second man to win four Indy 500s, Unser is a three-time national champion who ranks behind only A J Foyt and Mario Andretti in national championship wins (39) and, together with A J and Mario, is the only driver to win championship races on paved ovals, dirt ovals and a road course in a single season. He is also the only driver to win the Indy car "Triple Crown" of 500-mile races (Indianapolis, Pocono and Ontario) in a single season (1978).

In contrast to older brother Bobby's fiery style, Al is known for his patient, smooth driving that, often as not, has seen him emerge as a potential winner in the closing stages of the event. A versatile driver, Unser was also a major force in the Formula 5000 and Can-Am road racing series in the 1970s and, of course, the Pikes Peak hillclimb. Reduced to part-time duty since 1986, Al has remained a threat in selected races and, indeed, won his fourth Indy 500 in 1987 only after a last minute decision by Roger Penske to enter a car for him. And in addition to his other accomplishments, Al is the proud father of Al Unser Jr, whom he beat for the 1985 national championship by a single point.

## Indy car heroes: Rick Mears

One of the most popular drivers in Indy car history, Rick Mears was the unassailed master of the speedways before his surprise retirement at the end of the 1992 season. A three-time national champion, Mears became the third man to become a four-time winner of the Indianapolis 500 and he stands alone as the only driver to win the Indy pole six times.

During his career, Mears won eight 500-mile Indy car races in 41 starts, just one less than A J Foyt, who started nearly 70 Indy car 500s between 1958 and 1992. Articulate, unassuming and always accessible, Mears also set the standard for media and fan relations.

After making his start in off-road racing, Mears drove second-rank Indy cars for a spell before Roger Penske signed him to substitute for Mario Andretti while he raced in Formula One in 1978. Mears took full advantage of the chance by earning Indy 500 "Rookie of the Year" honours. He scored the first of his four Indy wins the following year and never looked back.

Although rightfully known for his successes on the ovals, Mears was also a skilled road racer. He is the only man to win all the road races in a single Indy car season and he lapped faster than World Champion Nelson Piquet in a test with the Brabham F-1 team. Mears suffered horrendous injuries to his feet and ankles in a crash in 1984, however, and most of the wins in the latter part of his career came on ovals and speedways.

Since his retirement, Mears has stayed on with the Penske team, serving as a liaison between the engineering staff and drivers Paul Tracy and Emerson Fittipaldi.

## USAC PAVES THE WAY

In the wake of the horrific crash that claimed more than 80 lives during the 1955 24 Hours of Le Mans, the AAA bowed out of the race-sanctioning business, and the newly formed United States Automobile Club (USAC) took over in 1956. Although USAC did little to change the rules, the club did begin to expand the national championship series to additional paved ovals which had cropped up in places like Darlington, South Carolina, Trenton, New Jersey and Phoenix, Arizona, in addition to Milwaukee, which had paved its former dirt track.

## WHEN TWO WORLDS COLLIDE...

A curious sidelight to the national championship occurred in 1957 and '58 when Italian promoters organized the Race of Two Worlds, which pitted America's top drivers and machinery against the best Europe had to offer at Monza's 2.6 mile high banked oval. The Americans, born and bred oval racers, were blessed with high-powered roadsters specifically designed for the job. Led by Jimmy Bryan and Jim Rathmann, they overwhelmed the comparatively feeble opposition organized by the promoters, although Stirling Moss did manage to win a heat race in a Ferrari.

European racing was to extract its revenge in spadefuls. It began innocently enough, when wealthy entrepreneur Jim Kimberly convinced Jack Brabham to bring his World Championship-winning Cooper Climax to Indianapolis for a test in the autumn of 1960. With its 2.5 litre engine, the

Cooper was grossly underpowered in comparison to the 4.2 litre, 400 horsepower Offenhausers that dominated Indy at the time, but the nimble rear-engined Cooper enabled Brabham to lap at an encouraging 144.8 mph – about two mph slower than the fastest speeds of the 1960 race.

Emboldened, Brabham and Cooper came back for the 1961 Indianapolis 500 with a larger 2.8 litre engine, finished an encouraging ninth, but then promptly forgot about further triumphs at the Brickyard.

## BRITS AT THE BRICKYARD

Another Englishman by the name of Colin Chapman was watching intently, however, and entered three cars based on the successful Formula One Lotus 25 monocoque chassis in the 1963 Indy 500. In addition to the revolutionary chassis, the Lotus effort was backed by a "spare no expense" Ford factory engine programme which produced an aluminium version of its Fairlane V-8 for Indianapolis.

On the way to his first World Championship, Jimmy Clark nearly won the 1963 Indy 500, coming in second only after a controversial decision by USAC officials not to black-flag Parnelli Jones' roadster, which was losing oil at a prodigious rate in the latter stages of the event. Later that year, Clark would score the first victory for a rear-engined car when he won the pole and dominated the August race at the Milwaukee Mile.

Clark dropped out of the 1964 Indy 500 (pictured below) with suspension damage caused when his Dunlop tyres began to disintegrate, leaving A J Foyt to win the roadster's swan song. Clark won in dominant style in 1965, completing with Chapman and Lotus (pictured right in 1966), the rear-engined revolution started by Brabham and Cooper. Exit the roadster.

*Although the Brickyard is not known for welcoming "outsiders" with open arms, Clark and Chapman are widely revered figures at the Indianapolis Motor Speedway.*

The following year Indianapolis was dominated by the British as never before – or since. After a monumental accident on the first lap eliminated a third of the field, Clark led for long stretches but dropped back after a couple of spins. His place at the front was taken by fellow Scotsman Jackie Stewart, who looked like a sure winner until he was felled by a drivetrain failure just ten laps from the finish. Stewart walked back to the pits to thunderous applause as his team-mate on the BRM Formula One team – Graham Hill – took the chequered flag to become the first rookie to win the Indianapolis 500 since George Souders in 1927.

Ironically, Jackie never raced again at Indianapolis. But Clark and Hill were back in 1967, both retiring early and leaving Formula One honours to be upheld by "kiwi" Dennis Hulme, who finished fourth. But Lotus wasn't the only Formula One constructor represented at Indy in 1967. The Brabham name was back, not as a driver but in the form of the Brabham BT25, which retired after 108 laps in the hands of future World Champion Jochen Rindt.

## ESSENTIAL ENGLISH ENGINEERING

Although F-1 drivers would lose interest in Indianapolis in the ensuing years, a number of constructors kept up the British influence at the Brickyard. Chapman came back in 1968 and '69 and, after Lotus disappeared from the scene, McLaren came in force as constructor and entrant throughout the '70s. Lola also joined the fray and became the first – and only – chassis to win Indy car racing's "Triple Crown" of 500 milers (Indianapolis, Pocono, Ontario). By then the Cosworth DFX engine had arrived to dominate the '70s and '80s.

---

### Indy car heroes: Bobby Unser

*Alternately cantankerous, charming and mischievous, Bobby Unser was a tough-as-nails racer who more than made up for any shortcomings in talent by sheer tenacity. As a result he won the Indianapolis 500 three times, the national championship twice and 35 national championship races in his 33-year career. His third Indy 500 win, in 1981, was shrouded in controversy after Bobby was initially penalized for improperly rejoining the race after a pit stop. After four months of legal wrangling, Unser was reinstated to what was, ultimately, his final Indy car win.*

*Notorious for fiddling with his race cars in search of the slightest mechanical advantage, Unser started from pole in 15 of 21 races in 1971 and '72 with Dan Gurney's All American Racers team. He also made an abortive attempt to drive in Formula One with the BRM team in 1968. Some of Bobby's greatest achievements, however, took place in the annual Pike's Peak hillclimb, where he won no fewer than 13 events, including ten overall victories, and set a dozen records in the process.*

## TURBINE TECHNOLOGY IN THE '60s

By the late 1960s the Indianapolis establishment had another revolution to contend with: the turbine. Taking advantage of a generous loophole in the USAC rules book, Andy Granatelli commissioned the construction of a four wheel drive chassis powered by a Pratt & Whitney ST6 turbine. The turbine offered significant advantages over piston-driven engines, including a favourable power-to-weight ratio (the ST6 weighed in at 260 pounds and was rated at 550 horsepower), excellent fuel economy and a rising torque curve which resulted in tremendous acceleration.

Parnelli Jones was recruited to drive the Granatelli turbine in 1967 and he utterly dominated the race before a

*Stewart's solo speedway:* Jackie Stewart starts the long walk back to the pits (opposite) after dropping out of the lead in the 1966 Indianapolis 500 less than 25 miles to the finish. The fact that he was accorded Rookie of the Year honours – despite the fact that fellow rookie Graham Hill actually won the race – is a measure of the respect Stewart earned in his only appearance at the Speedway.

transmission failure put him out of the race less than ten miles from the finish. USAC reacted by slapping heavy restrictions on the air intake of turbine engined cars for 1968. Granatelli responded by commissioning Chapman to build Lotus chassied-turbines for 1966 Indy 500 winner Graham Hill, Art Pollard and Joe Leonard to drive. In the race, Pollard and Hill retired early and Leonard's fuel pump failed while he was leading the closing stages of the race, paving the way for Bobby Unser's first win.

Popular as the turbines may have been with the technology freaks of the day, USAC had little choice but to restrict their performance further – or face the likelihood of making 99% of the existing Indy car equipment obsolete. However, a major development that did take hold in the late '60s was the appearance of turbocharged Offenhauser and Ford engines. Although the Fords were not initially competitive, the Offenhauser took to turbocharging quite readily and won in 1968, thus giving the venerable Offy another lease of life.

## SPEED UNLEASHED IN THE '70s

Aerodynamics were also beginning to get attention in the late 1960s, despite a USAC rule limiting body height and requiring any aerodynamic aids to be incorporated into the body shell. Gordon Coppuck, designer of the successful McLaren M23 Formula One car, stretched the USAC rules to the breaking point in designing the M16 Indy car for the 1971 season and when the USAC rules were relaxed for 1972, an unprecedented escalation in speed was unleashed.

Ever since Rene Thomas had shattered the 100 mph barrier at Indianapolis in 1919, speeds had been edging upwards at an inexorable rather than meteoric pace. "Gentleman" Jack McGrath was the first pole winner to top 140 mph in 1954; it took eight more years for Parnelli Jones to better 150 mph and AJ Foyt broke 160 mph in 1965. Peter Revson's pole-winning speed of 178.696 in 1971 was a full eight miles per hour faster than Al Unser's speed of the year before. But when the aerodynamic rules were freed up for 1972, Bobby Unser obliterated every existing standard with a staggering four-lap average of 195.940 mph in his Eagle-Offy.

Together with the relaxation in aerodynamic rules, the science of turbocharging had progressed to the point where engines such as the Offenshauser and the Foyt (AJ's development of the original aluminium Ford) were putting out in excess of 1000 horsepower in qualifying trim. While the speeds kept going up, unfortunately, safety did not always keep pace. The equation finally careened out of balance in the dreadful month of May, 1973, when drivers Art Pollard and Swede Savage were fatally injured in crashes, mechanic Armando Teran died in an accident in pit lane and, most horrific of all, Salt

26

**Dapper driver** *Graham Hill (top) became a crowd favourite at Indianapolis after his surprise win in 1966. Although an early retiree in 1967, he was in contention for a repeat of his earlier triumph in 1968 (above) in his STP Lotus turbine when he hit the Turn Two wall.*

## Indy car heroes: Johnny Rutherford

"Lone Star JR" has been racing Indy cars for some 30 years and, in that time, has won three Indy 500s, a total of 27 championship races and the 1980 PPG championship. A graduate of the Texas modified circuit, Rutherford made his first national championship start in 1962, and won his first Indy car race in 1965. His big break came in 1973, when he joined McLaren's Indy car team, and he won his first

Indy 500 the following year, repeating this success in the rain-shortened 1976 race. After joining forces with fellow Texan Jim Hall on the Chaparral team in 1980, JR won his third Indy 500 (seen here on his way to Victory Lane with hitcher Tim Richmond) and four other events to capture the PPG title.

Without a full-time ride, Rutherford subbed for the injured Rick Mears at Michigan in 1984 and set a closed-course record of more than 215 mph to earn the pole. Michigan was also the site of JR's last win, when he narrowly edged Mexico's Josele Garza to take the 1986 Michigan 500 and become – at 47 – the oldest 500-mile race winner in Indy car history. An utterly fearless competitor, Rutherford's classy off-track demeanour has made him popular with fans and sponsors. In recent years, JR has also tried to qualify for his 25th Indianapolis 500, but success has eluded him.

Walther crashed in the opening lap of the race, spraying burning methanol into the jam-packed grandstands.

USAC reacted by limiting the amount of turbo boost on engines, restricting wing size and location and limiting the amount of fuel carried on board to 40 gallons. Thus speeds at Indianapolis and other venues dropped and the safety record improved in the mid-'70s.

Andretti, the Unsers (Al and Bobby) and A J Foyt dominated the national championship in the 1960s and '70s with Foyt winning an unprecedented seven national championships, Andretti three and the Unsers a total of three. "Pelican" Joe Leonard, a former motorcycle racer, won back-to-back titles in 1971 and '72 while Tom "The Gas Man" Sneva, a former junior high school principal, duplicated that feat in 1978 and '79 and in 1978 also became the first man to win the Indianapolis pole at a speed of more than 200 mph.

### MID-'70s: CHANGES AND CRISES

By the mid-'70s, the national championship was contested almost exclusively on paved ovals. The advent of the rear engined race cars had further distanced the dirt tracks from the Indy 500 and, with an increasing number of paved oval facilities – including the vast Indianapolis clone at Ontario, California as well as new speedways at Pocono (Pennsylvania), Texas and Michigan – the dirt ovals and the Pikes Peak

Having missed the 1969 Indy 500 after breaking his leg in a motorcycle accident in the paddock, Al Unser roared back to take the first of two consecutive Indy 500 victories – and four overall – in 1970.

Hillclimb were dropped from the USAC national championship. Fittingly, the last man to win a national championship event at Pikes Peak was Mario Andretti; the last man to win a dirt track race that counted for the national championships was Al Unser.

All was not well with the national championship, however. In the face of the skyrocketing costs associated with turbocharged engines and new chassis every year (in the glory days of the roadster a single chassis could be competitive for years), static purses and virtually no voice in the key decisions affecting their sport, a group of team owners headed by Roger Penske and Pat Patrick petitioned USAC for additional input at the Board of Directors level. When they were rebuffed in 1978, the restless team owners broke away from USAC to form their own association – Championship Auto Racing Teams (CART) and announced their own series for 1979. In keeping with their intention to improve the marketing of Indy car racing, CART also announced a national television package for their new series.

The following seasons were turbulent ones. First, the CART team owners' entries to the USAC-sanctioned 1979 Indianapolis 500 were denied. The CART owners prevailed in a civil suit, and as the rival USAC Indy car series subsequently struggled to attract representative fields, the CART series grew. Sponsorship was acquired from PPG Industries for the full 1980 CART series, although an attempt to run Indy car racing under a joint CART/USAC organization called Championship Racing League failed. This left the CART-

### Indy car heroes: Michael Andretti

*In company with Al Unser Jr, Michael Andretti carried the standard for a second generation of Indy car drivers in the 1980s and '90s. Mario Andretti's eldest son, Michael, got his start in go-karts and Formula Fords before moving up to increasingly powerful equipment, finally making his Indy car debut in the last races of the 1983 season. Although it took Michael a few years to find his feet in Indy cars, his career took off in 1986 when he won three races and became the first driver to earn one million dollars in a single season of Indy car racing. He joined his father at Newman/Haas Racing in 1989 in the first father/son driving team in Indy car history and developed into one of the most forceful drivers in the sport.*

*Despite numerous wins and poles, Michael was denied in his efforts to capture the PPG title, finishing second in 1986, 1987 and 1990 before putting it all together in 1991 with eight poles and eight victories in 17 races. 1992 was another year of statistical domination for Michael, as he led more than half of all racing laps but finished a close second to arch-rival Bobby Rahal in the PPG points. All told, in 1991 and 1992 Andretti led 2101 of 4227 racing laps in Indy car competition. A quiet, even shy man away from the race track, Michael experienced a rough baptism in Formula One in 1993, but those who witnessed him running wheel-to-wheel at 220 mph with Rick Mears in the 1991 Indianapolis 500 have no doubts about his ultimate abilities and threat to Mansell in '94.*

**Route 66**: *Mark Donohue (no. 66) was to Roger Penske what Jim Clark was to Colin Chapman. Penske's driver from 1966 until his tragic death after a crash in practice for the 1975 Austrian Grand Prix, Donohue was at the wheel of the first of Penske's nine Indianapolis 500 wins in 1972.*

sanctioned PPG Indy Car World Series standing alone as the descendant of the national championship series first begun by the AAA more than 60 years earlier. For its part, USAC continued to sanction the Indianapolis 500 as well as hundreds of sprint car, midget and associated dirt track races throughout the country.

## THE '80s: DRIVEN BY DIVERSITY

The initial PPG Indy Car World Series bore a striking resemblance to previous USAC series in that it was heavily weighted to the historic paved ovals at Phoenix, Milwaukee and Trenton, with additional dates at the new super speedways in California, Texas and Michigan. Gradually, however, the focus of the PPG series moved from an oval-based series to a diverse mixture of venues. In part this was a function of CART's efforts to diversify its audience base. However, it also reflected the hard times faced by the oval facilities as Trenton, Ontario, Texas and Michigan, which were closed down – it was only Roger Penske's intervention that saved Michigan International Speedway from the wrecker's ball. New road racing circuits were added in the form of Road America, Mid-Ohio, Laguna Seca and Riverside, while temporary circuits were established at Cleveland's Burke Lakefront Airport and the Meadowlands Sports Complex just west of New York City.

Fittingly, Penske driver Rick Mears won the initial CART series in 1979, while Johnny Rutherford took full advantage of the first "ground effects" Indy car – the Chaparral 2K – to

win the 1980 championship. Like so many modern race car principles, ground effects – which use channels of air passing beneath a car in a manner that literally "sucks" the car to the ground – was pioneered by Colin Chapman in Formula One when Mario Andretti won the 1978 World Championship. Mears rebounded to win again in 1981 and '82 in Roger Penske's initial "ground effect" chassis, while Al Unser narrowly edged Italian Teo Fabi to win the 1983 PPG title.

## EARLY-'80s: THE ENGLISH EQUATION

By the mid-1980s, Indy car fields had grown substantially, due in large part to the marketing efforts of CART but also to the evolution of English-based March Engineering as a supplier of affordable, competitive chassis. In addition, since 1976 a turbocharged development of the remarkable Cosworth V-8 Formula One engine – the DFX – had been winning Indy car races with regularity. Again, the DFX was readily available to anyone who had the requisite finances. So in the early 1980s, a would-be Indy car team owner could easily (if not inexpensively) acquire the basic tools needed to win races.

And many did. In addition to long-time Indy car stalwarts Penske and Patrick, new teams cropped up like weeds – Provimi, Shierson, Forsythe, Galles, the Machinists Union – while the Truesports and Newman/Haas teams forsook their road racing roots to go Indy car racing. And when Newman/Haas went Indy car racing it was with another brand of customer chassis as Carl Haas was a long-time importer for Huntingdon-based Lola Cars. While Pat Patrick and Roger Penske continued to build their own chassis, known respectively as Wildcats and Penskes, Patrick eventually gave in to customer cars, leaving Penske to go it alone. Even Penske, however, was forced to buy March chassis on a couple of occasions when his own chassis (built at the Penske shop in Poole, Dorset) proved uncompetitive.

## LATE-'80s: THE CHASE FOR CHEVY

Under the chairmanship of John Frasco, who argued CART's case against USAC at Indianapolis in 1978, the PPG series continued to expand, adding new venues and dates at a torrid pace through the mid-1980s. But there were storm clouds brewing.

The kit car equation that had spurred the dramatic growth of Indy car racing began to unravel when two ex-Cosworth engineers by the name of Mario Illien and Paul Morgan wooed – and received – the backing of Roger Penske and Chevrolet to design and produce a new Indy car engine. Although it suffered through a lengthy gestation period, Ilmor's (a combination ILlien and MORgan) Chevrolet Indy V-8 eventually became the dominant engine in Indy car racing, winning 53 of 55 races between 1988 and '91.

The problem? Owing to Ilmor's limited capacity, not every team that wanted a Chevrolet Indy V-8 could get one. And with Cosworth slow to react, there was no viable alternative to teams not on the Chevy list. John Judd produced a variant of his Honda-based V-8 and won a single race in 1988, while Porsche's multi-million dollar Indy car programme achieved exactly the same thing – one win in three years of effort. At that they did better than Alfa Romeo, which entered the series in 1988 and failed to win a race, indeed never even gained a podium finish in three seasons of trying.

## TO HAVE AND HAVE NOT

Although the supply of Chevrolet engines was being increased incrementally each year, not surprisingly, the new engines generally went to the teams best able to put Chevrolet's racing effort in the most favourable light – in other words, the richest teams. There were, however, more "have not" teams than "haves". The "have nots" – led by veteran labour activist Andy Kenopensky of the Machinists Union team – were angered at what they perceived as favouritism on the part of Frasco and the Board of Directors towards the "haves", and succeeded in replacing Frasco and revamping the Board of Directors structure to give every team owner a vote in key decisions affecting CART.

Former Playboy licensing president Bill Stokkan was named CART's Chairman and Chief Executive Officer in early 1990. Stokkan was charged with improving CART's marketing efforts and improving the series' commercial viability. Almost simultaneously in Indianapolis, Tony George – the grandson of Tony Hulman – was named president of the Indianapolis Motor Speedway.

## INTO THE '90s

Meanwhile, on the track Al Unser had defeated his son – Al Unser Jr – by a single point in 1985 to win the closest national championship in history, while Bobby Rahal and Truesports Racing won two successive championships in 1986 and '87 before Danny Sullivan won Roger Penske's sixth PPG title in 1988. The following season, Emerson Fittipaldi completed a remarkable comeback from his post-Formula One retirement by winning both the Indy 500 and the PPG title in one of the most successful seasons in Indy car history.

But a new generation of drivers was also coming to the fore. Al Unser Jr struck a blow for youth by winning the first PPG title in the 1990s for Galles/Kraco Racing. He was succeeded by his long-time friend and rival, Michael Andretti, who led nearly half the racing laps on his way to the 1991 title for Newman/Haas Racing. And in 1992, Bobby Rahal scored an upset victory of sorts by winning the title in his first year as a team owner after acquiring the assets of Patrick Racing – in conjunction with partner Carl Hogan – in the off-season.

1992 also marked the introduction of the new Cosworth XB engine, produced in association with the Ford Motor Company. Although lightning fast, owing to its compact design and greater fuel efficiency, the Ford/Cosworth was not always

as durable as the now-venerable Chevy Indy V-8 and so while Michael Andretti again dominated in poles and laps led, it was Rahal's Chevy that was around at the finish most often.

1992 also saw the emergence of a host of talented young drivers such as Canadians Scott Goodyear and Paul Tracy, who engaged in a spirited duel at the Michigan 500 that finally went the latter's way, while the even younger Robby Gordon also emerged as a major talent.

Off the race track, CART continued to expand into new markets. After adding two Canadian races to the schedule in the form of the Toronto and Vancouver street races, CART travelled to Surfers Paradise, Australia for the Gold Coast Grand Prix in 1990 and, later, reached an historic agreement with FISA that future international expansion of Indy car racing would be confined to oval tracks. On the home front, the Meadowlands temporary course was abandoned after a succession of promoters were unable to turn a profit at the uninspiring track but, on a more positive note, two new ovals

were added to the schedule in recent years: Nazareth Speedway and New Hampshire International Speedway.

CART also dissolved its unwieldy 24-vote Board of Directors in favour of a five-man Board, with Stokkan and George as non-voting members. The inclusion of George on the CART Board signalled a thaw in the cold war that had existed between the Indianapolis Motor Speedway and CART since the 1978 schism.

While much work remains to be done in bringing CART, USAC and the Speedway together into a harmonious working unit, mid-1993 saw CART and USAC agree on a common rules package up to the 1997 season – tangible recognition that the sport can only benefit from cooperation on all sides.

***Towering trophy***: *Presented to the winning driver of the Indianapolis 500, the Borg Warner trophy (left) was cast from 80 pounds of sterling silver and cost $10,000 when it was made in 1936. The trophy, which carries busts of all the Indy 500 winners, is on permanent display at the IMS Hall of Fame Museum. Race winners, such as Fittipaldi in '89 (below), receive a two foot high sterling silver replica, mounted on a walnut plaque.*

# THE RHYTHM OF THE RACE

Like a travelling circus in the 1800s, the teams of the PPG Indy Car World Series criss-cross North America from April through to October, bringing their show to race tracks and cities from Long Beach to New Hampshire, from Toronto to Vancouver, along with a trip to Australia's Gold Coast. While each race is completely different, there's a common rhythm to every event, beginning when the massive transporters start rolling into town a day or two before the race.

Thursday is usually a busy but relaxed day, devoted to setting up the work area in the paddock as well as the nearby hospitality units which will be used to entertain current and would-be sponsors. The on-track action starts on Friday, with a morning practice session followed, on the road courses, by the weekend's first qualifying session. Friday night is a time to prepare for Saturday, making the adjustments needed to go faster or, for the unfortunate, repairing any damage.

## Practice and qualifying
On Saturday the pace intensifies, as this will be the final chance to ensure a good starting position. Morning practice is a series of two or three lap spurts, followed by a call in the pits where drivers and engineers discuss possible ways to make their car faster, and mechanics swarm over the machinery to inspect it for any problems and, later, make the subtle changes that may translate to vital fractions-of-a-second on the track. Qualifying is more of the same, with drivers and team managers searching for just the right moment – when there's a break in traffic, when the chassis set-up has been optimized, when the tyres have reached their peak efficiency – to go for a time.

Just as the pace and tension intensify with each passing day, so does the spectator interest. Friday's

heroes in action before the crowds arrive, are joined on Saturday and Sunday by the weekend fans as well as hundreds of corporate VIPs who fly in to town to see their cars in action.

The tension builds once more on Sunday as the supporting Firestone Indy Lights race goes off a couple of hours before the main event and continues to mount during lunch, a final time for fans to catch a favourite driver for an autograph or picture in the paddock. The excitement peaks as the traditional call goes out: "Ladies and gentlemen, start your engines."

## The pace is set
Then it's time for the PPG Pace Cars to lead the field around to the start, the most dangerous, action-packed moment of any motor race. Once underway, an Indy car race normally boils down into distinct segments broken up by pit stops every 65 to 70 miles for fuel and tyres. Positions can change dramatically during pit stops owing to any of a hundred problems ranging from a jammed wheel nut to a recalcitrant fuel nozzle. Then too seemingly minor adjustments to the car's aerodynamic settings can also have a significant impact on performance and, following the pit stops, cars that were previously struggling can almost magically gain speed and vice versa.

## Stratagems and spectators
The pit stops and full course yellows – being the colour of the flag which is waved whenever there's an incident on an oval, or a dangerous situation on a road course – keep the racing close and entertaining. But such race tactics also demand the most of the teams and drivers who must stay one step ahead of the competition in terms of strategy. Equally, the fans have to pay close attention in order to try and read the minds of the

**M**ore like a microwave setting, the liquid crystal display panel relays all relevant data to the driver inside the all carbon-fibre Indy car cockpit. The microwave comparison is not fanciful. Note the temperature reading: during three hours of racing this can rise to 150° with no cooling via the drivers' three-layer flame-resistant suit, balaclava and full-face helmet. No wonder they can lose up to 6% of their body weight in this intensely heated environment. The steering wheel (removed here) is quick-release for ease of access. The cockpit opening can be squeezed to a mere 30in x 14¾in minimum. All Indy cars must also have a built-in operable fire extinguishing rig – in case things get too hot to handle!

**T**ypically razzmatazz graphics cover the sides of Chevrolet's support trailer that is present at every Indy car race. The trailer houses an impressive array of computer equipment used to monitor the performance of the Chevy–powered cars during practice and qualifying. Each team has its own support trailer, housing a machine shop and ancillary equipment that can cost anything between $250,000 – $750,000.

The Galles Racing team unloads the cars of Kevin Cogan (foreground) and Al Unser Jr from their 18 wheel transporter. In addition to hauling race cars around the country, the transporters also carry spare cars, engines, wheels, and disposable spare parts worth $½ million alone.

▼ Lap top for lap stop: a Walker Motorsport team engineer checks the Ford Cosworth engine settings on Hiro Matsushita's Lola with the aid of portable computer technology. Between practice and qualifying, engineers, drivers and mechanics work hard together to get the best engine performance, car alignment, ride height and weight distribution.

**M**ethanol for Mansell: the most noticeable – and dramatic – difference in pit stops between Indy car and Formula One racing are the two helmeted fuel operatives (seen here pumping Nigel Mansell's Newman-Haas Lola). A crack pit crew can change four tyres, pump 40 gallons – the maximum fuel capacity – of methanol into the car, and give the driver a quick drink, in less than 15 seconds. Unlike Formula One, Indy car racing limits the number of people who can work on a car during a pit stop to six – one for each tyre, one to refuel the car and another to manage the fuel vent.

Kenny Bernstein looks on as Roberto Guerrero brings his Budweiser-King Lola Chevy into the pits in practice. One of America's most successful racers, Bernstein is a four-time drag racing champion and the first man to break the 300 mph barrier in the quarter mile, as well as owner of NASCAR and Indy car teams. In 1992, Roberto Guerrero, driving Bernstein's Quaker State Lola Buick, won the Indy 500 pole position with a record-breaking and unbeaten 232.482 mph.

**T**hree-time PPG Cup champion (1986/1987/1992) Bobby Rahal corners his Miller Genuine Draft Lola–Chevy; note the bubble containing a television camera on the nose of the car. The 1993 Season was watched by over ¼ billion viewers worldwide in over 90 countries.

Canadian Paul Tracy changes from rain tyres back to slicks on a drying track at Portland. Tracy, the young gun of 93, finished 3rd in his Penske PC22-Chevrolet Ilmor C, after 102 laps, behind Nigel Mansell and the winner Emerson Fittipaldi. If it rains on an oval track, the race won't take place. At road course events such as this, the Chief Steward can call a "dry start" when drivers choose to start on wet or slick tyres; or a "wet" start when all cars must start on rain tyres.

Former F-1 World Champion and four time National Champion Mario Andretti discusses tactics with friend, team co-owner, and Oscar-winning actor Paul Newman. "The guy is a racer himself," says Mario (Newman has four Sports Car Club of America national titles), "his contributions to the team's success are much more than you might believe."

Al Unser Jr – the only driver to score points from every race of the 1992 season – storms out of the pits at Portland after changing to rain tyres midway through this 7th race of the season. He finished 5th.

The start of the mid-season race! Paul Tracy and Nigel Mansell lead the field into the first corner of the 10-turn, 2.369-mile temporary road course at Cleveland. Unlike Formula One, Indy car racing uses rolling starts. Tracy eventually won comfortably after 85 laps, with Mansell – despite a sprained wrist – finishing third in a tremendous wheel-to-wheel tussle behind Emerson Fittipaldi. This course is Indy car racing's fastest road circuit.

**W**hoops! Bobby Rahal (black suit), Roberto Guerrero and Championship Auto Race Teams' officials examine the aftermath of a collision in the first hairpin turn at Cleveland. For local favourite Rahal, and for Guerrero, it was the end of the race. Several laps later, Paul Tracy regained the lead over Nigel Mansell on that same hairpin and led for the rest of the race.

Indy car Safety Team officials attend to Scott Goodyear after an off–track excursion. At each race there are over 20 safety, medical and rescue personnel and a state-of-the-art mobile intensive care centre for any on-track incidents.

In his aptly numbered Newman-Haas Lola, Mario Andretti finished the Portland race in 6th position – a lap behind team-mate Nigel Mansell in 2nd place. The car numbers are allocated as follows: No.1 goes to the previous PPG Cup champion (Bobby Rahal) while Nos. 2-12 are awarded to the entrants according to the previous season's performance (Mario was 6th overall in 1992). Mansell's No. 5 came via a swop by team owner Carl Haas of Michael Andretti's No. 2 for Derrick Walker's/Scott Goodyear's No. 5 – a welcoming gesture, too, to Mansell's F-1 "Red 5". Superstition dictates there is no No. 13; and No. 14 is reserved for AJ Foyt Jr – the all-time Indy car winner with 61 victories. By this stage, Mario had notched up 52 Indy car wins – the 2nd all-time winner.

Emerson Fittipaldi's daughter Tatiana joins her father, Paul Tracy and Nigel Mansell on the victory podium in Portland, Oregon. Portland, north of California on America's West Coast, was Round 7 of the 16-race series. At this stage Mansell led the world series by 14 points over Raul Boesel, followed by Emerson Fittipaldi, Mario Andretti and Paul Tracy. By the next race – midway in the 1993 season – Tracy had led more laps than any other driver and had moved up to 4th position.

**S**moke signals the end: Robby Gordon manoeuvres quickly from his smoking AJ Foyt/Copenhagen Racing Lola T92-Ford Cosworth XB during the 2nd Indy car race at Phoenix. A former dune-buggy and off-road truck driver, Gordon still managed to finish 18 after 104 laps in the race itself. Having come 3rd on Australia's Gold Coast, the opening race, Robby was very much in contention early in the 1993 season.

The chequered flag not only signals the race's end, it is the green flag for the teams to begin breaking down their pit equipment, and loading up their transporters and motor homes so that they can get an early start for the next destination, never more than a couple of weeks, and never less than several hundred miles, away.

# PENSKE RACING

The standard by which other Indy car teams are judged, Penske Racing has been the most successful team in the sport for more than two decades. Indeed, with gaudy statistics like more race wins (71), Indy 500 wins (8), poles (100) and championships (8), Penske is arguably the most successful team in the history of Indy car racing.

Penske Racing effectively started in the late 1950s when Roger Penske, then a student at Lehigh University, raced his Corvette in local hill climbs. After graduating from Lehigh, Penske's driving career blossomed to the point that he was named driver of the year by prestigious *Sports Illustrated* magazine and competed in the 1962 US Grand Prix.

Penske retired from driving in 1965 to launch a hugely successful entrepreneurial career, one which began as sales manager of a Philadelphia Chevrolet dealership and has since grown to encompass a string of auto dealerships, Penske Truck Leasing, two race facilities (Michigan International Speedway and Nazareth Speedway) and Detroit Diesel, builders of heavy equipment engines. With annual revenues of more than $2.8 billion, Penske Corporation currently employs more than 10,000 people at 400 facilities worldwide.

While he was building his business empire, Penske nurtured his own professional racing team; indeed he used his team's success to augment his business growth. Together with driver Mark Donohue, Penske Racing won the United States Road Racing Championship (forerunner of the Can-Am series) and then was one of the few to challenge the all-conquering McLaren Can-Am teams of the late '60s and early '70s. Penske Racing introduced the Porsche 917 turbo to the Can-Am

series in 1971 and won the '71 and '72 titles.

By that stage, however, Penske was already involved in Indy car racing, having first entered the Indianapolis 500 in 1969. It took five tries, but Penske and Donohue won the 1972 Indy 500. The team went on to several more Indy car wins in the mid-1970s, even as Penske branched out into stock car and Formula One racing. Penske Racing established its own chassis manufacturing operations in Poole, Dorset, but suffered a tragic setback in 1975 when Donohue was killed practising for the Austrian Grand Prix. A year later, John Watson won the Austrian Grand Prix for Penske, but the team abandoned Formula One at the end of the season to focus on Indy car racing.

With driver Tom Sneva, Penske won the national championship in 1977 and again in 1978 after the team switched its manufacturing effort to Indy cars. Although the early Penskes were little more than modified McLarens, the team would ultimately design and build its own chassis to tremendous effect. Also, in 1978, Penske hired little-known Rick Mears to fill in for Mario Andretti while the veteran pursued the World Drivers Championship.

At the same time, Roger Penske was among the leaders of a group of Indy car team owners who formed a new sanctioning body – Championship Auto Racing Teams – in response to what they perceived to be the administrative failures of the United States Auto Club. In time, this body took over the sanctioning of the entire Indy car series with the exception of the Indianapolis 500.

Meanwhile, Mears was winning three races in 1978, three more in 1979

*Esprit de corps: Two of the driving forces in Indy car racing – Penske Racing and Emerson Fittipaldi – joined forces in 1990. The result has been more than half a dozen wins, including the 1993 Indianapolis 500.*

(including the Indy 500) and his first national driving title. Rick went on to win another driving title in 1981 and a third in 1982. Al Unser won the PPG championship in 1983, making it five straight wins for Penske, then came back after a down season to win another PPG title in 1985, making it seven national championships in nine seasons for Penske Racing.

With Mears winning a second Indy 500 in 1984 and Danny Sullivan winning

his first for Penske in 1985, Penske Racing was the dominant force in Indy car racing. Sullivan would go on to win the 1988 PPG title while Mears won two more Indy 500s – in 1988 and '91 – before announcing his retirement at the end of the 1992 season.

Although Penske Racing won more than a dozen races between 1982 and 1986, it was not without some difficulties. Although the Penske PC10 chassis of 1982 was a worldbeater, its successors from PC11 to PC16 ranged from mediocre to horrible. Never one to let ego get in the way of success, Penske quickly switched to the customer chassis produced by March Engineering

and won the '84 and '85 Indy 500s as well as the 1985 title in a customer car.

In 1987 Penske hired designer Nigel Bennett from Lola and his PC17 won both the 1988 Indy 500 and PPG titles; the following season, Bennett's PC18 duplicated that feat, albeit for Patrick Racing after Penske agreed to sell a limited number of Penske chassis to his rival.

Meanwhile, Penske was also breaking ground on the engine front, in concert with Chevrolet, underwriting the efforts of Ilmor Engineering to produce a worthy challenger to the dominant Cosworth DFX engine. Although the Chevy suffered teething

problems in the 1986 and 1987 seasons, it became the dominant powerplant from 1988 to 1992 – winning five straight Indy 500s and five straight PPG titles. And after long association with sponsors Pennzoil and Miller Beer, 1990 saw Marlboro join Penske as its primary sponsor – a relationship that has spelled success for both parties.

Mears' retirement in 1992 marked the end of an era for Penske Racing. But with twice World Champion and 1989 Indy 500/PPG champion Emerson Fittipaldi on board, together with talented youngster Paul Tracy, Penske Racing is quite prepared to enter a new era in Indy car racing.

1993 marks the start of the second decade for the unique partnership between Oscar-winning actor (and accomplished racer) Paul Newman and Carl Haas, arguably the most prolific figure in American auto racing. The son of German immigrants, Haas raced sports cars himself in the 1950s before becoming North American importer for Lola Cars. In partnership with Jim Hall's Chaparral team, Haas won three SCCA Formula 5000 championships in the 1970s, while winning four championships in the Can-Am series with his own team and a virtual Who's Who of international drivers from Jackie Stewart to Alan Jones, Jacky Ickx, Patrick Tambay and Peter Revson.

When Haas and Lola decided to go Indy car racing in 1983, Carl persuaded Newman (then associated with a rival Can-Am team) to join the venture, with more than a little assistance from the team's driver (Mario Andretti) and primary sponsor – Budweiser beer. Newman/Haas Racing struggled in 1983 with the Lola (dubbed the "Slowla") but scored their inaugural victory at Road America. The following season, Newman/Haas won six of 16 races and clinched the PPG championship in the final race of the season.

The team went on to score nine more wins in the next four years, as the Budweiser sponsorship gave way first to Beatrice and, later, Kmart

*Hats off to Haas...and Newman: In Australia, Nigel Mansell joined Mario Andretti, Alan Jones and Jackie Stewart as World Champions who have driven for Carl Haas. Known for his "trademark" unlit cigar, Haas' profile could hardly be described as "low key", (even against Paul Newman) especially as he is also SCCA's Chairman of the Board, CART and Road America Board Member, importer of Lola race cars and race organizer of the Milwaukee Mile.*

department stores and Texaco/Havoline. Then in 1989 Newman and Haas put together one of the most intriguing driver pairings in history when Michael Andretti joined the team. Although the team suffered some growing pains in 1989, Michael won two races. Michael scored five wins the following season but had to concede the PPG title to the equally prolific but more consistent Al Unser Jr. And 1991 was all Newman/Haas as Michael swept to eight wins, eight poles and led more than 45% of the season's racing laps. Although Newman/Haas won the statistical battle again in 1992, with five wins, eight poles and 55% of the laps lead, they again had to settle for second best in PPG points.

By that point, however, Michael had accepted an invitation to drive for the McLaren F-1 team. Within days of his Formula One deal, Carl Haas was negotiating with leading Indy car drivers, including Al Unser Jr, about replacing Andretti. But Haas also had a bombshell up his sleeve in the form of World Champion designate Nigel Mansell, who made the unprecedented decision to move to Indy car racing after his own negotiations with the Williams Formula One team broke down. Thus Haas, who has never been shy about employing European drivers, scored one of the most significant coups in racing history, when he announced that Mansell would team with his one-time team-mate Mario Andretti for the 1993 season. To orchestrate the Mansell/Andretti line-up, Haas hired veteran team manager Jim McGee, whose Indy car resumé features more than 30 wins as a chief mechanic and several national championships, the most recent being the 1992 PPG title with Rahal/Hogan Racing.

# RAHAL/HOGAN TEAM MILLER

At once one of Indy car racing's newest teams and one of its oldest, Rahal/Hogan managed to meld three separate entities together – Bobby Rahal, Carl Hogan and the remnants of Patrick Racing – in its first year of existence to win the 1992 PPG Indy car World Series.

Little more than five months before the start of the 1992 season, what would become Rahal/Hogan Racing was more recognizable as Patrick Racing International, the descendant of Patrick Racing, one of Indy car racing's most successful teams in the 1970s and '80s. Formed by oil exploration tycoon Pat Patrick, the team won 29 races from 1973 through to 1988 – including two Indy 500s and one national championship – many using the team's own "Wildcat" chassis. Patrick sold controlling interest in the team to Chip Ganassi in 1989 and, still operating under the Patrick team name, won the Indy 500 and five races with Emerson Fittipaldi to claim its second national title.

In 1990, Patrick team manager Jim McGee and engineer Morris Nunn formed Patrick International in partnership with Alfa Romeo, and entered Alfa-powered cars for two seasons before parting company with the Italian auto maker at the end of 1991. At the same time, they signed Rahal as their driver for 1992, without any firm commitments from a competitive engine manufacturer to replace Alfa. Indeed, Patrick's relationship with Chevrolet had soured before his move to Alfa and with no engine available to Patrick himself, he was forced to offer his team to Rahal.

Rahal, a two-time PPG World Series Champion and a successful businessman in his own right, had been discussing the possibility of eventually forming his own team with trucking magnate Carl Hogan. A successful entrant in the Can-Am and Formula 5000 series of the 1970s, Hogan had expressed interest in some day joining forces with Rahal. When the opportunity to acquire the assets of Patrick for 1992 came up, Hogan jumped at the chance. Former Patrick sponsor Miller Beer supported the move to the hilt and Rahal/Hogan Racing was born.

While keeping the nucleus of the former Patrick team, Rahal and Hogan quickly added their own touch to the organization. When Truesports Racing announced it would cease operations at the end of 1992, Rahal – who had won the 1986 and '87 PPG titles with Truesports – convinced a number of his former associates to join Rahal/Hogan. At mid-season, Rahal and Hogan announced plans to move the team from their Indianapolis base to the former Truesports facility near Columbus, Ohio. And in the autumn, Rahal and Hogan decided to pursue Truesports' "Made in America" chassis project, which featured the only Indy car chassis designed and built in the United States, in cooperation with the Ohio State University wind tunnel.

*The view looks good: A mainstay of the Can-Am and F-5000 series, trucking magnate Carl Hogan returned to the front line of motorsports as a co-owner of Rahal/Hogan Racing in 1992.*

# GALLES RACING INTERNATIONAL

Although Galles Racing has been one of Indy car racing's most successful teams in the 1990s, the Albuquerque, New Mexico-based team also has a volatile legacy. Formed by Rick Galles – whose family has widespread real estate and automotive dealership holdings in the Southwest – Galles Racing's fortunes have often been linked with those of another Albuquerque family – the Unsers; specifically, Al Unser Jr.

Galles formed his racing team around Unser in 1981 and went after the SCCA Super Vee Championship, a "training ground" series for small, open wheel cars powered by 160 hp Volkswagen engines. Galles Racing dominated the series in 1981, winning the championship, then moved to the 800 horsepower Can-Am series and promptly won that in 1982.

Galles and Unser made their Indy car debut in 1983 and finished seventh in the PPG points on the strength of two second place finishes and a number of other strong showings. The following season, Galles and Unser scored their first Indy car win at Portland but Al subsequently joined Shierson Racing in 1985 while Galles continued with a multi-car effort featuring Geoff Brabham, Roberto Moreno and Pancho Carter. Although Brabham came close to winning on several occasions, ultimate victory eluded him and at the conclusion of the 1987 season, Unser and Galles announced they were joining forces again with increased sponsorship from Valvoline.

Although the team used a March 88C chassis, (which proved markedly inferior to both the Lola T88/00 and Penske PC17s of 1988), Galles tied the PPG Series champion Penske team with four wins in the year thanks, in large part, to the effective working relationship developed between Unser

and engineer Alan Mertens. After nearly winning the Indy 500, only to see Unser crash after a last-second shunt with Emerson Fittipaldi, the team had an off season in 1989. At mid-year, however, it was announced that Galles and Kraco Racing team owner Maurice Kraines would join forces for 1990, a pairing that would bring Unser and Kraco driver Bobby Rahal under the same roof.

In its first year, Galles-Kraco was a resounding success as Unser scored six wins, including a World Series record four straight wins at mid-season, to claim the PPG title while Rahal came home fourth in the points. Although 1991 saw Rahal and Unser finish second and third to Michael Andretti, the seeds

*Getting it right: Having shelved their Galmer chassis project at the end of 1992, Galles Racing re-joined the Lola fold this year. After initial struggles, both Danny Sullivan and Al Unser Jr visited the victory lane.*

of discontent had been sown with Rahal, who jumped to Patrick Racing at the end of the year. Galles/Kraco responded by quickly signing Danny Sullivan to a multi-year contract while simultaneously announcing plans to build its own chassis, in cooperation with Galmer Engineering, itself a joint venture between Galles and Mertens.

Although the Galmer chasis sat on the pole for its first race (the Gold Coast Grand Prix), won its third race (Long Beach) and scored an improbable victory in the Indianapolis 500, lack of resources and development saw the Galles/Kraco entries slip down the finishing order as the season progressed. Galles ultimately shelved the project at the end of 1992 and ordered Lola T9300 chassis for the current season. Meanwhile, Kraines bowed out of his partnership with Galles, who subsequently signed Molson beer as primary sponsor for Danny Sullivan's car.

# A J FOYT ENTERPRIZES

# WALKER MOTORSPORT

In terms of longevity and achievement, Houston-based A J Foyt Enterprises is one of the greatest in Indy car history. After tremendous success as a driver in the 1950s and early '60s, Foyt struck out on his own in the mid-1960s with his own team and, eventually, his own chassis (the Coyote) and his own engines (Foyt/Fords). Foyt won five races, including his third Indy 500, to claim his fifth national championship in his Coyote in 1967 and went on to 29 more wins by the end of the 1970s.

Foyt won only one race in the 1980s – the poorly supported, USAC-sanctioned 1981 Pocono 500 – and as his results tapered off, so did the quality of his team. Although A J's irascible personality and indefatigable driving occasionally brought the team up to competitive speeds, Indy car racing's increasing professionalism generally left Foyt Racing behind. Although the team regularly qualified two, three and four cars for the Indianapolis 500, they were rarely running at the halfway point, let alone the finish.

After Foyt suffered grievous injuries in a crash in 1990 at Road America, he began taking a more active role in the day-to-day administration of the team. He placed several respected individuals such as crew chief John Anderson and, more recently, engineer Ken Anderson (no relation), in positions of responsibility. He and sponsor Copenhagen also brought in a number of up-and-coming drivers for try-outs and settled on Robby Gordon as their driver for 1993.

Owner Derrick Walker cut his racing teeth as a mechanic on the Brabham Formula One team and, later, as manager of Roger Penske's plant in Poole, Dorset. Later he was team manager of Penske's Indy car effort from 1980 through to 1988 – a span of time that included five Indy car titles, five Indy 500 wins and 28 other Indy car wins.

Walker parted company with Penske to become team manager for the Porsche Indy car programme and battled long odds in '89 and '90 with the team, eventually scoring a win at Mid-Ohio in 1989 and pole at Denver in 1990 before Porsche disbanded its effort.

*Thoroughbred: All-time Indy car champ AJ Foyt retired at Indianapolis after a driving career spanning five decades.*

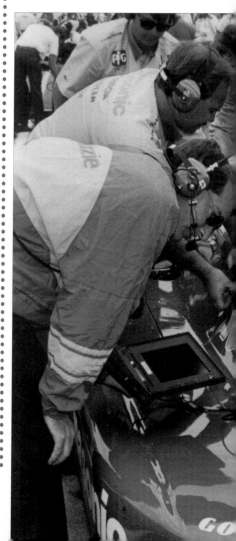

56

Unphased, Walker organized his own operation in 1991 with which Willy T Ribbs became the first African-American to qualify for the Indy 500. Early in 1992 Walker reached an agreement with the Mackenzie Financial Corporation to take over its Indy car programme with driver Scott Goodyear. Although the team had a slow start, Goodyear eventually came home a brave second at Indianapolis and went on to win the Michigan 500 and finish fifth in PPG points. For 1993 Walker expanded first to a two-car effort, when Hiro Matsushita and sponsor Panasonic were added to the team, and later added a third car for Ribbs with support from the Service Merchandise department store chain and actor Bill Cosby.

*Expansion: Hiro Matsushita joined Walker Motorsport after two seasons with Dick Simon Racing.*

# HALL/VDS RACING

The partnership of Jim Hall and Count Rudy van der Straten brought two of racing's most illustrious figures together when they announced the formation of their Indy car team in 1990. Hall, legendary creator and driver of the Chaparral sports cars and, later, Indy cars, was returning to racing after a seven year absence. Van der Straten's cars had won in everything from European F-5000 races to the Can-Am championships, and his VDS engine building shop was synonymous with excellence.

Hall/VDS Racing got off to an auspicious start, with John Andretti coming through to win the team's inaugural race in the first Gold Coast Grand Prix. Andretti and Hall/VDS enjoyed considerable success in 1991 and '92, but the Pennzoil car failed to win another race and for the current season the Midland, Texas based outfit named Teo Fabi as its driver.

*Searching for form: Hall/VDS Racing started off with a bang in 1991 by winning their first race at Surfers Paradise but have struggled to regain winning form since. For 1993 they replaced John Andretti with Teo Fabi, winner of five Indy car races since 1983, but failed to find the winning touch. Here team members check out practice times and performances.*

# DICK SIMON RACING

# BETTENHAUSEN MOTORSPORTS

Look for the word "survivor" in the dictionary and you just might find a picture of Dick Simon. The former insurance industry executive, champion skydiver and race car driver has made a living keeping his Indy car team not just alive but growing against all odds. And in recent years, Simon Racing has shown very definite signs of joining the big boys.

Simon left a successful career in the insurance industry to try his hand at racing and made his Indy car debut in 1970, finishing third in the California 500. Entering his own car over the next 18 seasons, Simon finished in the top five a total of five times in 177 races and earned more than $1.5 million. He began fielding cars for other drivers in the mid-1970s, and was instrumental in helping Janet Guthrie become the first woman to qualify for the Indianapolis 500 in 1976. Simon later introduced Raul Boesel, Scott Pruett, Ian Ashley, and others to Indy car racing.

Simon retired at the end of 1988 to concentrate on running his team, which fielded cars for Arie Luyendyk and Scott Brayton in 1989. After Luyendyk departed, the team concentrated on an Amway-sponsored one car effort for Brayton at most races but expanded to two cars in 1990 with the addition of Hiro Matsushita. 1992 was Simon's best season as Boesel replaced the injured Matsushita at Indianapolis and went on to score ten top-ten finishes and finished tenth in the PPG points despite missing the first three races of the season.

In the off-season, Simon reached an agreement with Duracell batteries to sponsor Boesel's car in 1993. He also entered into a partnership with Jim Hayhoe's fledgling team – which entered eleven Indy car races in 1992. Thus in addition to the cars of Boesel, Brayton and occasional driver Lyn St James, Simon is also co-entrant for Jimmy Vasser's car in 1993.

Like many Indy car team owners, Tony Bettenhausen is a racing driver himself. But unlike Roger Penske, Carl Haas, Chip Ganassi, Jim Hall and Dick Simon he's not quite ready to describe himself as a retired racing driver. Tony's introduction to racing actually came long before he ever drove a race car, for he is the youngest son of two-time national champion Tony Bettenhausen, who was killed in a crash at Indianapolis in 1961.

Following his father's death, Tony and his brothers Gary and Merle all followed Tony Sr's footsteps and became racing drivers. After sampling stock car racing, Tony went Indy car racing in 1979 and was named USAC Rookie of the Year. After several years of driving for other teams, Bettenhausen formed his own team in 1986 – with the help of friends and acquaintances – and gradually built his programme to a professional level, acquiring sponsorship from the Amax metals and mining conglomerate in 1990 and culminating in 1992 when he arranged to purchase chassis from Penske Racing.

After a disastrous May in which he crashed and failed to qualify for the Indy 500, Tony stepped out of the cockpit and offered Stefan Johansson a ride in the Detroit Grand Prix. Johansson responded with a brilliant drive to second and went on to finish 14th in the PPG standings despite starting just nine races. Bettenhausen solidified his status as one of Championship Auto Racing Teams' up-and-coming team owners by signing Johansson for the '93 season and acquiring new chassis from Penske, the first to do so since Patrick Racing won the 1989 PPG title with Penskes.

Unfortunately, the many promising elements assembled by Bettenhausen for 1993 failed to produce much in the way of results.

*Against the odds: A former insurance company executive and champion skydiver, Dick Simon (below, right) had his finest year as a team owner in 1993.*

# BUDWEISER/KING RACING

Kenny Bernstein is no stranger to success or speed, as his four NHRA (National Hot Rod Association) drag racing titles attest. In fact, Bernstein is one of the few Indy car team owners who can argue he's gone faster – much faster – than his driver as he was the first drag racer to break the 300 mph barrier in 1992.

In addition to his own driving career, Bernstein owns a successful NASCAR Winston Cup stock car team and fielded Buick's official Indy 500 entries from 1988 through to 1992. Bernstein's car earned the Indy 500

pole in 1992, with Roberto Guerrero clocking a four lap average of 232.482 mph, but fell out of the race in ignominious fashion when Guerrero crashed on the pace lap. At the conclusion of the 1992 season it was announced that Bernstein would field an Indy car team for the entire 1993 season, sponsored by Budweiser beer.

*No job security here: Budweiser joined forces with drag racing star Kenny Bernstein's Indy car team in 1993. Although Roberto Guerrero (pictured) was competitive on the mile ovals, he was off the pace on the road and street circuits and was replaced by Eddie Cheever after the Vancouver race.*

59

# CHIP GANASSI RACING

A former Indy car driver, Chip Ganassi was fastest rookie qualifier for the 1982 Indy 500 and was named "Most Improved Driver" of 1983. Driving for Patrick Racing, he suffered a near fatal accident in 1984 and eventually retired.

Ganassi later acquired a controlling interest in Patrick Racing and went on to win the Indy 500 and the PPG title before a somewhat acrimonious split with Patrick. In a busy first year under the Chip Ganassi Racing name, Ganassi attracted sponsorship from Target department stores and hired Formula One refugee, Eddie Cheever, who promptly won Indy 500 and CART "Rookie of the Year" honours to compliment a ninth place finish in the PPG standings. The team finished ninth again in the '91 standings and slipped to tenth in 1992, failing to win a race. Near the end of the '92 season, Cheever was notified his contract would not be renewed and Arie Luyendyk, who drove for Ganassi in the Indy and Michigan 500s, was named as replacement.

*Mixed fortunes: 1993 was the best and worst of times for driver-turned-team-owner Chip Ganassi. His car won the pole and finished second at Indianapolis, but was generally uncompetitive elsewhere. At season's end he announced that Michael Andretti would drive for him in 1994.*

## ARCIERO RACING TEAMS, INC

Frank Arciero is one of the legendary names in American racing, having entered cars for men like Phil Hill (America's first Formula One champion), Dan Gurney and Al Unser in sports cars races in the 1950s and '60s. Arciero, a successful Southern California real estate contractor and developer, has regularly fielded Indy car teams since the early 1980s with intermittent success, nearly winning the Cleveland Grand Prix in 1983 and finishing third in the 1987 Indy 500 with "Rookie of the Year" Fabrizio Barbazza (who drove for the Minardi F-1 team in 1993).

In recent years, however, Arciero devoted his energies to his burgeoning vineyards in central California, but the arrival of Mark Smith, sponsorship from Craftsman Tools and the acquisition of '92 Penske-Chevies for the 1993 season heralded his return as a major player on the Indy car scene.

## DALE COYNE RACING

Another racing driver turned team owner in the mould of Dick Simon, Dale Coyne has literally pulled himself up by the bootstraps to become a respected figure in Indy car racing. Coyne began his own racing career in 1985 and moved to Indy car racing in 1986 with a low budget operation featuring second and third hand equipment.

Despite widespread criticism of his uncompetitive equipment, Coyne persevered and, after stepping down as a driver, began running an increasingly professional operation for a succession of drivers including Dean Hall, Paul Tracy and, in 1993, Robbie Buhl.

60

# EUROMOTORSPORT RACING

**Hard tryer:** *Antonio Ferrari (left) introduced a couple of bright young talents to Indy car racing in 1993, including F-3000 star Andrea Montermini and California's David Kudrave (shown here, centre).*

A distant relation of the legendary Enzo Ferrari, Euromotorsports team owner Antonio Ferrari raced cars in the Italian Formula Three championship and F-3000 before coming to the United States. Euromotorsport Racing ran virtually a full season with year-old cars in 1989 with driver Mike Groff and, at Indianapolis, Davy Jones, who finished seventh after qualifying 31st.

Ferrari continued to enter cars in '91 and '92, scoring several top ten finishes in the process.

# LEADER CARDS RACERS

Indy car racing's longest-lived team, Leader Cards Racers, dates back to the 1950s when Rodger Ward and crew chief AJ Watson won two Indy 500s and three national championships with the team. Owned by Ralph Wilkie, whose Milwaukee-based Leader Cards fine paper product company the team takes its name from, the team also won the 1967 Indy 500 with Bobby Unser but thereafter went into a decline.

Although Wilkie and Watson continued to field Indy car entries throughout the 1970s, '80s and into the '90s, increasing costs left them further and further behind. After missing much of the 1992 season, however, the team was rejuvenated when former Indy car driver Bob Lazier entered into a partnership with Wilkie and planned an ambitious season with his son Buddy driving for the team.

## CONTENDING TEAMS

# PRO-FORMANCE MOTORSPORTS

One of Indy car racing's newest teams, Pro Formance Motorsports is owned by Tim Duke, (whose Pro Formance Driving School provides performance driving experiences to automotive industry executives), and John Dick, who worked as race engineer for a number of Indy car teams, including Shierson Racing in 1990 when that team won the Indy 500 with driver Arie Luyendyk.

A start-up organization in 1993, the team planned a limited schedule with two 1990 Lolas and driver Scott Pruett.

# TURLEY MOTORSPORTS

Former Long Beach policeman Norm Turley was a long time supporter of the Indy Lights series through his P I G (Personal Investment Group) Team, which also fielded Indy cars in 1990, '91 and '92 for driver Ted Prappas.

Following the conclusion of the 1992 season, Turley announced that he was forming his own team featuring driver Eddie Cheever and '92 Penske Chevrolets.

61

*Elusive points: Norm Turley acquired 1992 Penske Chevies for the season, but results were few and far between for drivers Eddie Cheever and Brian Till.*

# CHAMPIONS AND CONTENDERS

## WHAT MAKES AN INDY CAR DRIVER?

America is often called the great melting pot of humanity. It is altogether fitting then, that its national driving championship is contested by drivers from all walks of racing life, both from North America and around the world. The starting field for the 1993 Indy 500, for example, included four former World Champion drivers, four more with Formula One experience, a one time off-road racer, several more who cut their teeth on America's midget and sprint car circuits, and others who got their start in domestic sports car racing. In the last ten years, Indy car winners have hailed from Brazil, Canada, Italy, Colombia, Holland, Mexico, the United States and Texas (just kidding).

## HIT THE DIRT TRACK

It was not always thus. Although "foreign" drivers occasionally played a part in the national championship prior to World War II, the post-war period was dominated by American drivers who were born and bred on the bullrings of America, starting in a bewildering variety of cars and classes but almost always graduating to Indianapolis via midget and what have come to be known as sprint cars. Although that dirt-track experience may not have been the ideal training ground for learning how to drive on the macadam of the Indianapolis Motor Speedway, the balance of the national championship was contested on dirt tracks from Sacramento, California to Syracuse, New York.

## LEADING FROM THE REAR

That began to change with the introduction and eventual domination of the Formula One-based rear engined cars in the 1960s, together with the increasing number of paved ovals and road courses that began to make up the national championship schedule. Manhandling a 700 horsepower sprint car around the bullrings of the Midwest became increasingly irrelevant to a championship which, by 1969, consisted of ten

*Famous faces: Former World and Indy Car Champions acknowledge "rookie" Mansell's arrival. Left to right front row: Mario Andretti, Al Unser Jr, Scott Brayton, Kevin Cogan; second row: Raul Boesal, Emerson Fittipaldi, Danny Sullivan. Many expected Mansell to dominate the road courses and struggle on ovals, but ovals were his strong suit.*

paved ovals, eight road courses and just six events on dirt (including the Pikes Peak Hillclimb). Two years later, the national championship was contested exclusively on paved ovals.

Thus, team owners increasingly turned to drivers with rear engine, pavement experience. This led to an influx of drivers from the sports car ranks, skilled men like Peter Revson, Mark Donohue, George Follmer and Danny Ongais to be sure, but also a host of lesser lights who staked either their own personal money or that of commercial sponsors to "buy rides". In this respect, Indy car racing was no different to Formula One, where a host of "rich kid" racers descended on the World Championship in the mid-70s. But for every Niki Lauda and Peter Revson, there were half a dozen who had no business being behind the wheel of a potentially lethal race car.

**Different strokes for different folks:** Stefan Johansson (left) came to Indy car racing after a career in F-1, while Jimmy Vasser worked his way up through the American training ground system.

## THE ROUTES TO INDY

The demise of North America's two principal road racing series – the Can-Am and the Formula 5000 series – in the early '80s, coupled with Championship Auto Racing Teams' (CART) emergence as the sanctioning body of the Indy car series (and the subsequent growth of street and road races on the Indy car schedule), marked a sea change in the history of the Indy car driver. The influx of professional sports car racing teams such as Newman/Haas, Truesports and, later, Galles Racing, was accompanied by a similar invasion of established road racing drivers such as Bobby Rahal, Danny Sullivan, Kevin Cogan and Geoff Brabham.

At the same time, drivers whose careers had reached a dead end in Europe, began looking at Indy car racing as a viable alternative to Formula One. Thus Roberto Guerrero, Teo Fabi, and Derek Daly opted to pursue their careers stateside while Emerson Fittipaldi was lured out of retirement in 1984.

The success of CART also coincided with the development of the Super Vee and Formula Atlantic series as unofficial training grounds for aspiring Indy car drivers. Indeed, every Super Vee champion from 1978 to 1988 – including Brabham, Al Unser Jr, Michael Andretti, Arie Luyendyk and, most recently, Mark Smith – had a legitimate chance in Indy cars over the years while Formula Atlantic produced such standouts as Scott Goodyear and Jimmy Vasser.

By the latter half of the 1980s, though, the Super Vee series had commenced a decline that would see it disbanded following the 1989 season. At the same time, the Indy Lights class (aka the American Racing Series) – created by then-Indy car team owner Pat Patrick as a middle ground between the 215 horsepower Super Vees and the 700 horsepower Indy cars – was growing in fits and starts. The series ultimately produced its own success stories in Indy car racing drivers such as Indy Lights champions Mike Groff, Paul Tracy and Robbie Buhl.

## A DIVERSE SOURCE OF DRIVERS

Unlike Formula One, where drivers come through via a fairly regimented route from the various national Formula Three and the European Formula 3000 championships, Indy car racing boasts a driver line-up that is a reflection of a varied and, at times, confusing heritage. There are refugees from Formula One – from Nigel Mansell, Stefan Johansson, Teo Fabi, Roberto Guerrero and Eddie Cheever to Emerson Fittipaldi; there are products of the ARS/Super Vee training ground – Paul Tracy, Arie Luyendyk, Mike Groff, Mark Smith and Robbie Buhl; while others such as Mario Andretti, Al Unser Jr, Willy T Ribbs, Scott Pruett and Robby Gordon cut their teeth in everything from midgets and sprint cars to go-karts and sedans.

Meanwhile, this year's emergence of F-3000 star Andrea Montermini as a force in Indy car racing suggests that CART team owners will not necessarily confine themselves to ex-Formula One drivers when it comes to scouting European talent in the future.

# FORMER CHAMPIONS

# Nigel **MANSELL**

The first Englishman to win the World Driving Championship since James Hunt in 1976, Mansell is one of the most popular racing drivers in the world. Renowned for his fiercely determined, all-out style, Mansell came up just short of winning the World Championship in 1986 and 1987 and was christened "El Lione" by the Italian fans after winning his first race with the Ferrari F-1 team in 1988. After a falling out with Ferrari team-mate Alain Prost the following season, he announced his retirement but reneged on that when he was offered a spot with Frank Williams, with whom he ultimately won the 1992 title with a record-setting nine win season.

A native of a middle class family in Upton-on-Severn, Mansell began racing Formula Fords in 1976 and the following year won 32 of 42 starts. After breaking his neck in a shunt that season, Nigel checked himself out of hospital when the doctors told him to consider retiring. The following year he mortgaged his house to finance a four race Formula Three programme and earned a spot on the factory March team. After a couple of seasons in Formula Three and Two, Lotus signed him to an F-1 test contract and he eventually made his F-1 debut at the Austrian Grand Prix. There, Mansell set the tone for his Grand Prix career by driving much of the race with a fuel leak that left him with painful burns at the end of the race. Another noteworthy feature of that race is that his team-mate was none other than Mario Andretti.

Mansell drove full time for Lotus from 1981 through to the end of 1984 and although he failed to win, he earned several podium finishes as well as his first Formula One pole in the US Grand Prix at Dallas. That race was also memorable for the fact that Nigel collapsed while pushing his car to the finish line in searing heat after running out of fuel.

Nigel joined the Williams team in 1985 and scored the first of many popular homeground victories when he won the Grand Prix of Europe at

*The end of the road: Mansell and Frank Williams failed to see eye-to-eye on the 1993 F-1 season. The result? Mansell took his talents across the Atlantic.*

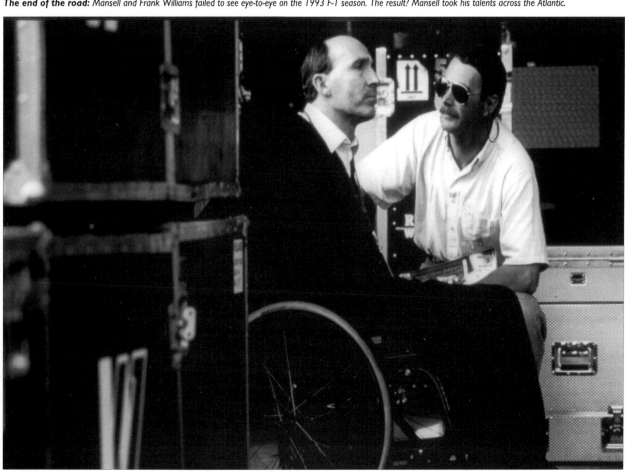

Brands Hatch and went on to finish sixth in the World Driving Championship. The following season Nigel lead all F-1 drivers in wins (with five, including the British Grand Prix, at Silverstone) and misfortune. On his way to the World Driving Championship in the final race of the year in Australia, Mansell's title hopes were derailed when a rear tyre blew out at 180 mph and he failed to finish the race.

1987 brought more success and more disappointment as Nigel again led the way in poles (eight) and wins (six) – including another win at Silverstone in which he passed team-mate and arch rival Nelson Piquet with just a few laps remaining – but failed to win the title. A crash during practice for the Grand Prix of Japan left Mansell with several crushed vertebrae and no chance to challenge Piquet for the World Driving title in the final two races.

Mansell went winless in 1988 after Honda took its business from Williams to McLaren, and he moved to Ferrari in 1989 to team up with three time World Champion Alain Prost. Nigel scored an historic win in his debut with the Prancing Horse in Brazil and followed that up with an equally brilliant win in Hungary, using lapped traffic to nip past Ayrton Senna. Although he won the Portuguese Grand Prix the following year, Mansell was upset with what he believed to be the favouritism shown to Prost within the Ferrari organization and he announced his retirement after dropping out of the British Grand Prix with mechanical problems.

Frank Williams, however, convinced him to un-retire – a task made easier when Nigel got a preview of the technical developments in the Williams pipeline. These developments included computer-activated suspension, semi-automatic transmission and traction control – together with Renault's full-fledged support. Although teething problems kept the Williams from showing its stuff in early 1991, Nigel came on like gangbusters in the final half of the year winning in France, Spain,

| Nigel Mansell |
| --- |
| **Born: 8-8-53,** |
| **Upton-on-Severn, England** |
| **Ht: 5'10", Wt: 167** |
| **Residence: Clearwater, Florida** |
| **Rookie Indy car season: 1993** |

Germany, Italy and (of course) England, but a botched pit stop in Portugal cost him any chance of overhauling Senna in the title chase.

1992 saw Mansell and Williams harvest the fruits of their efforts the previous season as Nigel won a record five races in a row to start the season. Although talk of him winning every race of the season went down the drain when a loose wheel dropped him to second at Monaco, Nigel added wins in France, England (naturally), Germany and Portugal and clinched the title in August – the earliest that had been done since 1971.

Mansell and Williams, however, were unable to reach agreement on a contract for 1993 and Nigel began entertaining other offers. One of the most intriguing came from Carl Haas, whose Indy car team had proved to be one of the most successful in the business in recent years. Haas and Mansell had talked previously when Nigel expressed an interest in Indy car

racing. When Haas made him a firm offer in early September and Williams continued to dither over a contract, Mansell took the Haas deal even though it promised substantially less money than anything then on the table with Williams. At the root of the problem between Williams and Mansell was the former's dealings with Prost, with whom Mansell had not got on at Ferrari; dealings encouraged by Renault.

The circumstances surrounding Mansell's departure from Williams only added to his popularity among the world's racing fans, who saw him as victimized by the unprincipled, predatory world of Formula One racing. Others, including much of the world's racing press, saw Mansell as a complainer who had repeatedly proved incapable of getting along with any team-mate.

Personalities aside, there is near-unanimous acknowledgment that Mansell is one of the world's fastest, bravest and skilled drivers. Any questions of that were quickly squashed by his near-instant adaptation to Indy car racing, where he won his first race and quickly adapted to oval track racing.

An avid golfer and close friend of Greg "The Shark" Norman, Mansell lives in Clearwater, Florida with his wife Rosanne and three children.

# Bobby **RAHAL**

The single most successful driver of the CART era, Rahal won back-to-back PPG titles in 1986 and '87 driving for the Truesports team, then won a third title in 1992 driving for his own team. Calculating and cold-blooded, Rahal is a driver who makes few mistakes on the race track and is no less adept as a businessman – as his string of auto dealerships and successful Indy car team attest. Indeed, some believe Bobby may one day be known more for his success as a team owner than as a driver.

That will take some doing, however. After starting amateur racing in 1975, Rahal joined the cut 'n' thrust world of the North American Formula Atlantic series in 1976, racing against the likes of Gilles Villeneuve and Keke Rosberg. He more than held his own and raced in the European Formula Three series in 1978 before landing a couple of end-of-season rides in the Canadian and US Grands Prix with Walter Wolf Racing.

Like many of his contemporaries, though, Rahal had nowhere to go in the United States and his career was at an ebb in the early 1980s when entrepreneur Jim Trueman decided to form an Indy car team. The marriage of Rahal and Trueman's Truesports Racing was a magical pairing. Rahal won two races in his rookie season of 1982, and went on to win the PPG title and the Indy 500 in 1986 – the latter just days before Trueman succumbed to his battle with cancer. Rahal and Truesports backed up their 1986 success with another title in 1987 and finished third in points in 1988. By then the relationship had run its course and Rahal jumped to the Kraco team, which merged with Galles Racing in 1990.

Although Bobby finished fourth and second, respectively, in the points in his two years with Galles/Kraco, he leapt at the opportunity to replace Sullivan at Patrick Racing for the 1992 season.

Although his long-term plans called for the creation of his own team, Rahal's timetable pushed forward when Pat Patrick was unable to secure a contract with a competitive engine supplier and offered to sell the team. Rahal quickly persuaded trucking magnate Carl Hogan to join him in a buy-out of Patrick, and Rahal/Hogan racing was born.

Many scoffed at Rahal's decision, but when he won the second race of 1992 at Phoenix it became clear that the Rahal/Hogan Racing would be a serious player sooner rather than later. And when Bobby won three more times, finished second three times, and amassed ten top three finishes he had not only secured his third PPG title as a driver, but his first as a team owner.

An avid golfer, Rahal sponsors the Bobby Rahal Columbus Charities Pro Am Golf tournament and owns Honda and Toyota/Lexus dealerships in Pennsylvania and Ohio.

| Bobby RAHAL | |
|---|---|
| **Born:** 10-1-53, Medina, Ohio | |
| **Ht: 6'1", Wt: 175** | |
| **Residence:** Dublin, Ohio | |
| **Rookie Indy car season:** 1982 | |
| **Indy car wins:** 24 (pre-1993) | |
| **Indy car poles:** 18 | |
| **Indy car earnings:** $11,166,578 | |

# FORMER CHAMPIONS

## Emerson **FITTIPALDI**

No man better epitomizes contemporary Indy car racing than Emerson Fittipaldi, a two-time world champion whose passion and commitment to auto racing have been reborn since taking up Indy car racing in 1984. The charismatic Brazilian has since become one of Indy car racing's most popular figures, and he shows no signs of slowing down as he nears 50.

Like Mario Andretti, Emerson's racing career began in partnership with his brother (Wilson), with whom he built and raced go-karts in his native Sao Paulo before moving to England in 1968 to race Formula Fords. In one of the most rapid rises to stardom in motor racing history, Emerson graduated to Formula Three in 1969 and, by mid-1970, was driving in Formula One for Team Lotus. He scored a memorable win in the US Grand Prix that year and went on to become history's youngest World Champion in 1972 on the strength of five wins in the JPS Lotus 72. After an unsuccessful title defence in 1973, he joined McLaren Racing in 1974 and promptly won his second World Championship.

The latter half of the 1970s, however, saw Emerson's star wane. In 1976 he formed the Brazilian-based Copersucar team and, while he was occasionally able to showcase his formidable talents, the project proved too much for him. He retired from driving in 1980 and, ultimately, disbanded the team after the 1981 season. Dispirited and in debt, Fittipaldi repaired to Brazil to make a new start with his citrus plantation holdings, Mercedes-Benz dealership and other commercial interests.

He came out of retirement in 1984 to drive a sports car in the Miami Grand Prix and, later that year, drove a couple of races for third rate Indy car teams before landing a ride with the Patrick Team. The following season, Fittipaldi's true form began to show as he stalked Mario Andretti and eventual winner Danny Sullivan throughout the Indy 500, and then won at fearsome Michigan International Speedway – at the time the fastest speedway on the Indy car schedule.

He won five more times in the next three years before a dream season in 1989 saw Emerson win the Indianapolis 500 and three of the next four races and clinch the PPG Indy car World Series Championship with a fifth win in October. By that point, however, he had already agreed to move to the Penske Racing team in 1990 and has since continued his remarkable string of success, winning at least one race each season and capturing his second Indy 500 this May.

| Emerson FITTIPALDI | |
|---|---|
| Born: 12-12-46, Sao Paulo, Brazil | |
| Ht: 5'8", Wt: 165 | |
| Residence: Sao Paulo, Brazil and Miami Beach, Florida | |
| Rookie Indy car season: 1984 | |
| Indy car victories: 17 (pre-1993) | |
| Indy car poles: 13 | |
| Indy car earnings: $9,093,158 | |

# Danny **SULLIVAN**

Either by serendipity or superb calculation – or a combination of the two – Danny Sullivan (*below, left*) was the ideal man to capitalize on the growth of Indy car racing in the 1980s. He began the decade a minor figure on the US racing scene, but on the strength of his driving and personal promotion skills, grew into one of America's most celebrated sports figures, as comfortable in a chic Hollywood restaurant or Aspen night club as he is hurling an Indy car through the Corkscrew at Laguna Seca Raceway.

Owing to the fickle fates of racing, Danny has not experienced the best of fortune on the track in recent years. Nevertheless, he remains a formidable opponent when he has competitive machinery at his disposal.

The start to Sullivan's racing career is shrouded in fable, from stories of racing impressario Frank Faulkner paying his tuition at the Jim Russell

Driving School at Snetterton, to Danny's days of supporting himself first as a lumberjack and later as a waiter and cab driver in New York City. After cutting his racing teeth in England in Formula Fords he moved back to the States to race Formula Atlantic and the Can-Am series before landing an Indy car ride in 1982. That gave way to a season of Formula One with Tyrrell Racing which begat a 1984 season with Doug Shierson's Indy car team – a season that produced three wins and an offer to drive for Penske Racing in 1985.

Sullivan jumped at the chance and quickly added to the lore of his career by winning the Indy 500. This was no ordinary Indy 500 win, though, for Danny won only after spinning a full 360 degrees while passing Mario Andretti for the lead. Miraculously, Danny kept his March 85C off the wall in what has been called one of the two greatest pieces of driving in Indianapolis history.

The other? Mario's miraculous miss of Sullivan's spinning car!

Danny eventually outlasted Andretti to win the race for Penske and begin one of Indy car racing's most successful alliances. He went on to several additional wins in '85, '86 and '87 before capturing the 1988 PPG title in impressive fashion, roaring back from three dnfs at the start of the season to win the title going away. He won twice more in 1989 and again in 1990, but by then sponsorship dynamics were at work that would ultimately force Sullivan to join the Patrick/Alfa Romeo team in 1991. Saddled with the anaemic Alfa Romeo V-8, Danny was rarely a factor that season but he rebounded to win the Long Beach Grand Prix in 1992 after moving to Galles Racing at the end of 1991.

| Danny SULLIVAN | | |
| --- | --- | --- |
| Born: 9-3-50, Louisville, Kentucky | | |
| Ht: 6', Wt: 165 | | |
| Residence: Aspen, Colorado | | |
| Rookie Indy car season: 1982 | | |
| Indy car wins: 16 (pre-1993) | | |
| Indy car poles: 19 | | |
| Indy car earnings: $7,623,970 | | |

## FORMER CHAMPIONS

# Mario **ANDRETTI**

In terms of longevity and diversity, Mario Andretti surely ranks among the greatest racing drivers in history. For more than three decades his name has been synonymous with automobile racing in the United States, while his essential humanity, unfailing honesty and willingness to answer the tough questions have made him a favourite with reporters.

Born in Trieste, Italy during World War II, Andretti spent much of his childhood in refuge camps before his family emigrated to the United States in 1955. Living in the Pennsylvania town of Nazareth, Mario and his twin brother Aldo began racing on the local dirt tracks in 1958. Although Mario soon graduated to increasingly professional forms of racing, Aldo was seriously injured in two separate crashes and retired in 1969.

The terror of United States Auto Club (USAC) midget and sprint car racing in the early '60s, Mario once won three midget features in a single day and was soon snapped up by one of the teams contesting the national championship. In this case, Clint Brawner, manager of the Dean Van Lines team, signed Mario to a contract in 1964.

The following year Mario won his first championship race on the road course at Indianapolis Raceway Park, finished third in the Indianapolis 500 to earn Rookie of the Year honours and edged A J Foyt to win the USAC National Championship. He retained the National Champion title in 1966, finished second in 1967 and 1968 and won again in 1969. Among his many victories in 1969 was the Indianapolis 500, a race in which he rebounded from a huge accident in practice to qualify second and beat two other American legends – Dan Gurney and Bobby

**Mario ANDRETTI**

| | |
|---|---|
| **Born:** 28-2-40, Montona, Italy | |
| **Ht:** 5'6", **Wt:** 160 | |
| **Residence:** Nazareth, Pennsylvania | |
| **Rookie Indy car season:** 1964 | |
| **Indy car wins:** 51 (pre-1993) | |
| **Indy car poles:** 65 | |
| **Indy car earnings:** $9,775,939 | |

Unser – to win auto racing's biggest prize.

Perhaps Mario used up all his good luck at Indianapolis in 1969, for he has yet to win a second time at the Brickyard. On occasions too numerous to mention, he has seemingly had the race in the bag only to be sidelined in the closing laps with mechanical problems. In 1987, for example, he led 170 of the first 177 laps only to suffer a broken valve spring less than 60 miles from the finish line.

Mario began branching out into other areas of the sport in the late '60s. In 1967, he stunned the stock car racing world by winning the Daytona 500 and followed that up by co-driving to victory in the 12 Hours of Sebring sports car race with Bruce McLaren. The following year he made a similar

impression on the world of Grand Prix racing, qualifying Colin Chapman's Lotus 49B on the pole at the US Grand Prix, his first Formula One race.

The 1970s saw Mario turn his attention to the world racing scene. He achieved a life-long ambition of winning a Grand Prix for Ferrari (in 1971, at South Africa) as well as numerous victories in the World Sports Car championship. But he suffered through some lean years in F-1 before the confluence of his talents and Colin Chapman's revolutionary "ground effects" chassis resulted in four Grand Prix wins for Lotus in 1977, followed by six wins and the 1978 World Championship.

Ironically, even as he was becoming the first American since Phil Hill to win the World Championship, Andretti's triumph was overshadowed by the death of his team-mate – Ronnie Peterson – at the Italian Grand Prix. Twenty-eight years earlier, when Hill clinched the championship at Monza, his team-mate – Wolfgang Von Trips – was killed that same day.

Mario refocused his attention on Indy car racing in the 1980s, as PPG Industries and the newly organized Championship Auto Racing Teams pumped new life (and money) into the sport. He joined a team formed by US racing kingpin Carl Haas and actor Paul Newman to drive a new Indy car designed by Lola Cars and, after a couple of learning years, the team went on to a torrid winning streak culminating in Mario's fourth national championship in 1984.

He went on to win ten more races in the 1980s and finished the decade with Newman/Haas and a new team-mate – his son Michael. Although he was overshadowed by Michael from 1989 to 1992, Mario continued to produce at an extraordinary level for a man entering his 50s: his win at Phoenix in the second race of 1993 – his 51st in national championship competition – was one of the most popular victories in Indy racing history.

# Al **UNSER Jr**

In a realm increasingly dominated by drivers with a background in domestic and international road racing, Al Unser Jr (*below, left*) is an anomaly. Not just a second, but a third generation racing driver in the fabled Unser family, Al Jr learned racing on the dirt tracks of America's Southwest under the eyes of his father Al (three time national champion) and uncle Bobby (twice national champion). Al was racing go-karts at the age of nine and sitting on telephone books to race 600 horsepower sprint cars at 16. By the time he was 20 he'd won the Can-Am series and made his Indy car debut, finishing fifth ahead of his father and AJ Foyt in the process.

He signed on with fellow-Albuquerquean Rick Galles to drive Indy cars full-time in 1983, moved to the Shierson team in 1985 and promptly came within a single championship point of winning the PPG title. The man who beat him? His father.

Al wouldn't come that close to a championship again for some time, but in the interim he established himself as one of the brightest stars in American racing by consistently finishing in the top three in the PPG championship while winning the International Race of Champions series in 1986 and 1988. He also established something of a record by dominating the Long Beach Grand Prix Indy car race, winning no fewer than four races in a row.

But more than Long Beach, the Indianapolis 500 is a race that utterly consumes Al Jr. No wonder. His father won the race four times, his uncle Bobby three times; and another uncle – Jerry – lost his life at Indianapolis in 1958. And Al came within inches of winning the 1989 Indy 500 – only to be punted into the wall in a desperate last minute confrontation with Emerson Fittipaldi. How much did that mean to him? When the Indianapolis Motor Speedway rebuilt its retaining walls in the winter of 1992, Al requested – and got – the section of wall he hit in 1989 and placed it in the backyard of his home in Albuquerque, New Mexico.

Al rebounded from the disappointment of the 1989 Indy 500 to win the 1990 PPG title going away, taking four wins in succession, six total. Yet, victory at Indianapolis continued to be elusive. The month of May offered Al little reason for optimism in 1992. Practice and qualifying indicated his team's Galmer chassis had little chance of matching the pace of the Lola-Fords of Mario and Michael Andretti, or the perenially strong Penskes of Rick Mears, Emerson Fittipaldi and newcomer Paul Tracy. But as car after car crashed on an unusually cold race day, Unser patiently worked his way to the front of the field. He took the lead when Michael Andretti's engine quit in the final miles, then held off a last lap challenge from Scott Goodyear to win the closest Indy 500 finish in history.

Rarely a spectacular qualifier, Al Unser Jr races in the spirit of his father, knowing full well the prize money and championship points are paid on race day, not in qualifying. He is easy on equipment and respected by his peers as a "fair" racer; but when the decisive moment of the race arrives, nobody is more agressive, more committed to winning than Al Unser Jr.

| Al Unser Jr | |
|---|---|
| Born: 19-4-62, Albuquerque, New Mexico | |
| Ht: 5'10", Wt: 150 | |
| Residence: Albuquerque | |
| Rookie Indy car season: 1982 | |
| Indy car victories: 18 (pre-1993) | |
| Indy car poles: 3 | |
| Indy car earnings: $10,711,590 | |

# John **ANDRETTI**

The son of Mario Andretti's brother Aldo, John is a chip off the old block, having cut his racing teeth on America's dirt tracks. Although people are quick to assume John's family name opened doors in the sport, they don't know about the thousands of miles he logged towing his midget race car around the country from race to race; or about his twice weekly commuting of nearly 1000 miles to attend Moravian College in eastern Pennsylvania while racing a USAC midget in Indianapolis on weekends.

After spending a season driving for BMW of North America in the IMSA sports car series, John got his break in Indy cars in 1987 when he replaced Tom Sneva on the Curb Racing team. He later joined the Porsche Indy car

team and then won his first race with Hall/VDS Racing in 1991 in the inaugural Gold Coast Grand Prix in Australia. John and Hall/VDS parted company at the end of 1992, though, and he found himself without a full time Indy car ride. Undaunted, he gave drag racing a try and advanced as far as the semi-final round in his first meet, recording a run at 298.70 mph in the process. He made a popular return to Indy car racing in the 1993 Indianapolis 500 driving for his godfather – AJ Foyt – and finished tenth after setting the sixth fastest qualifying time.

| John ANDRETTI | |
|---|---|
| Born: 12-3-63, Bethlehem, Pennsylvania | |
| Ht: 5'5", Wt: 135 | |
| Residence: Indianapolis, Indiana | |

| | |
|---|---|
| Rookie Indy car season: 1987 | |
| Indy car wins: 1 (pre-1993) | |
| Indy car poles: 0 | |
| Indy car earnings: $2,755,321 | |

# Teo **FABI**

Teodorico Fabi trained as an aeronautical engineer and raced motorcycles prior to his four-wheel career. The compact Italian burst on to the Indy car racing scene in 1983 by winning six pole positions and four races on the way to a second place finish in the PPG championship. Veteran racing fans were hardly surprised by his performance, however, as Fabi had an impressive record in European F-3 and F-2 racing and had driven for the Toleman F-1 team in 1982 after finishing second in the 1981 Can-Am series.

Fabi returned to Formula One from 1984 to 1987 driving for Brabham, Toleman and Benetton, before rejoining the Indy car fray with the Porsche team. He scored Porsche's only Indy car win at Mid-Ohio in 1989 but the team's

fortunes plummeted in 1990 and he found himself driving sports cars in 1991, winning the World Sports Car Championship with Tom Walkinshaw Racing. When Hall/VDS and John Andretti parted company in 1992, the call went out to Fabi.

| Teo FABI | |
|---|---|
| Born: 9-3-55, Milan, Italy | |
| Ht: 5'5", Wt: 140 | |
| Residence: Lamzada Sondrio, Italy | |
| Rookie Indy car season: 1983 | |
| Indy car victories: 8 (pre-1993) | |
| Indy car poles: 9 | |
| Indy car earnings: $2,362,012 | |

# Scott **GOODYEAR**

To many, Scott Goodyear stormed on to the racing scene in 1992 by starting last in the Indy 500 and falling just .042 seconds short of beating Al Unser Jr for the victory. Seasoned observers have marked the articulate Canadian out as a star of the future for quite some time, however.

A Toronto native, Scott is a national go-kart and Formula Ford champion who got his break in Indy cars in 1987 when he drove a handful of races for the underfunded Gohr Racing team. Despite showing promise, however, Scott found himself driving in the Rothman's Porsche Cup sedan series rather than Indy cars in 1988. However, a couple of "one-off" Indy car drives the following season

convinced Mackenzie Financial Services to back Goodyear in 1989.

After two more promising – but winless – seasons Goodyear and Mackenzie joined forces with Derrick Walker Motorsports for 1992. Their arrangement was put together at the last minute, so it took time for Goodyear and the Walker team to gel. But after their epic run at Indianapolis, Goodyear and Walker were one of the teams to beat in nearly every race for the remainder of the year, winning the Michigan 500 and finishing fifth in the PPG points.

| Scott GOODYEAR | |
|---|---|
| Born: 20-12-59, Boca Raton, Florida | |
| Ht: 5'7", Wt: 140 | |
| Residence: Toronto, Ontario, Canada | |
| Rookie Indy car season: 1987 | |
| Indy car victories: 1 (pre-1993) | |
| Indy car poles: 0 | |
| Indy car earnings: $2,568,033 | |

# Roberto **GUERRERO**

One of the most likable drivers in Indy car racing, Guerrero has experienced more than his share of racing's "highs" and "lows". A native of Medellin, Columbia, Roberto attended school in the United States before pursuing his racing career in England, first in Formula Fords and later in Formula Three. He graduated to Formula One in 1982 and '83, driving for the Ensign and Theodore teams, then moved to Indy car racing in 1984 where, together with Michael Andretti, he was named "Co-Rookie of the Year" in the Indianapolis 500.

After near misses, Roberto finally scored a memorable first Indy car win in 1987. He started the Phoenix race in last place after his qualifying time was disallowed due to a minor technical infraction but charged into the lead and won handily. He won again later in the

year at Mid-Ohio only to suffer near fatal head injuries a few days later in a crash while testing at Indianapolis.

He returned to Indy car racing in triumphant fashion, finishing a brilliant second at Phoenix in the opening race of 1988 but thereafter was never able to duplicate his performance. Set down by his team at mid-year he drove the underpowered Alfa-Romeo chassis for a couple of seasons, then stunned the racing community in 1992 with a brilliant four lap run to the Indianapolis 500 pole at 232.482 mph.

On top of the world one minute, Guerrero was down the next. On a bitterly cold race day, he crashed on the pace lap while trying to heat up his tyres. Team owner Kenny Bernstein stuck by his driver, however, and hired Roberto to drive for the Budweiser King Indy car team in 1993.

| Roberto GUERRERO | |
|---|---|
| Born: 16-11-58, Medellin, Columbia | |
| Ht: 5'8", Wt: 140 | |
| Residence: San Juan Capistrano, California | |
| Rookie Indy car season: 1984 | |
| Indy car wins: 2 (pre-1993) | |
| Indy car poles: 6 | |
| Indy car earnings: $3,586,948 | |

# Arie **LUYENDYK**

The free-spirited 40-year-old native of Sommelsdyk, Holland scored an unforgettable first Indy car win in 1990 when he passed Bobby Rahal with 33 laps remaining to win the Indianapolis 500. Although he went on to win two more races for Vince Granatelli Racing in 1991, Luyendyk was forced to sit on the sidelines much of the following year when Granatelli was unable to raise sufficient sponsorship to continue. He signed with Chip Ganassi Racing for a full season in 1993 and responded by winning his first pole position – once again at Indianapolis – and finishing a close second to Emerson Fittipaldi.

Luyendyk spent his childhood watching his father – Jaap – teach racing driving at the Zandvoort circuit, and followed his father's lead by winning the European Formula Ford and Super Vee titles before coming to the United States, where he won the 1984 Super Vee title. He moved to Indy cars in 1985, winning both CART and Indy 500 Rookie of the Year honours as well as 1987's Most Improved Driver award. Arie drove for Dick Simon racing in '88 and '89 before moving to Shierson racing in 1990. When Shierson sold his team, Granatelli took over the operation and the new combination won at Phoenix and Nazareth and came from last place to second in the Michigan 500.

An art aficionado, Luyendyk is owner of the Arie Luyendyk Motorsport Gallery in Indianapolis and is a national spokesman for the US Center for Missing and Exploited Children.

| Arie LUYENDYK | |
| --- | --- |
| Born: 21-9-53, Sommelsdyk, Holland | |
| Ht: 5'11", Wt: 160 | |
| Residence: Scottsdale, Arizona | |
| Rookie Indy car season: 1984 | |
| Indy car victories: 3 (pre-1993) | |
| Indy car poles: 0 | |
| Indy car earnings: $5,209,306 | |

73

# Paul **TRACY**

Great things have been predicted of this young Canadian from the moment he won the Canadian Formula Ford championship at 16 and followed that up a year later by becoming the youngest driver ever to win a Can-Am race. Along the way, Paul attended the Shannonville Racing Drivers School, where one of his instructors was a struggling driver by the name of Scott Goodyear. After a mercurial three years in the American Racing Series which culminated in the 1990 championship, Tracy was tabbed as a star of the future when Roger Penske hired him as a test driver for his Indy car team in 1991.

Although Paul crashed in his first race with Penske, he was scintillatingly fast in subsequent outings and stepped in for Rick Mears when injuries forced the four time Indy 500 winner to drive a reduced schedule in 1992. Often outqualifying team leader Emerson Fittipaldi, Tracy earned his first pole at Road America and scored a trio of top three finishes. With Mears' retirement, Tracy assumed full-time status in 1993.

Off track, Paul enjoys basketball and mountain biking. Restoring an Austin-Healey 3000 is another of his pastimes.

| Paul TRACY | |
| --- | --- |
| Born: 17-12-68, Toronto, Ontario, Canada | |
| Ht: 5'9", Wt: 168 | |
| Residence: West Hill, Ontario, Canada | |
| Rookie Indy car season: 1991 | |
| Best Indy car finish: 2nd (pre-1993) | |
| Indy car earnings: $699,702 | |

# Raul **BOESEL**

After more than a decade this native of Curitiba, Brazil has begun to emerge from the shadows of racing's "other" Brazilians – Emerson Fittipaldi, Nelson Piquet and Ayrton Senna. A former champion equestrian and engineering student, Boesel won his national go-karting title at the age of 17. He moved to England and won the 1980 RAC Formula Ford title and eventually drove for March and Ligier in Formula One.

When his Formula One career reached a dead end, Boesel looked to Indy car racing. He eventually persuaded Dick Simon to give him a test drive, which led to races with Simon in 1984 and '85. Boesel drove Jaguar prototypes for Tom Walkinshaw Racing in 1987 and won the World Sports Car Championship, then moved

back to Indy cars in 1988 with Shierson Racing. He later drove for the Truesports team and was inactive for much of 1991, but was reunited with Simon in 1992 when the team's regular driver – Hiro Matsushita – was injured at Indianapolis. Raul finished sixth at Indy, then came home second a week later in Detroit and finished tenth in the PPG points in what would be a prelude to even greater success in 1993.

| Raul BOESEL | |
|---|---|
| **Born:** 4-12-57, Curitiba, Brazil | |
| **Ht:** 5'7", **Wt:** 155 | |
| **Residence:** Miami, Florida and Curitiba, Brazil | |
| **Rookie Indy car season:** 1985 | |
| **Best Indy car finish:** 2nd (pre-1993) | |
| **Indy car poles:** 0 | |
| **Indy car earnings:** $3,228,319 | |

# Scott **BRAYTON**

This veteran campaigner has spent most of his racing career in Indy cars, after beginning his career racing go-karts in 1974 and later graduating directly into the PPG series from Formula Fords in 1981.

The son of former racing driver Lee Brayton, Scott has had several noteworthy moments in Indy cars, including setting a single lap qualifying record at Indianapolis in 1985 (speed, since broken) and leading several races, including both the Indianapolis and Michigan 500s.

After several years with low-budget outfits, Scott joined Simon Racing in 1988 and the pairing has made steady progress, with 1992 their best season to date. Scott reckons the most misunderstood aspect of Indy car racing

is the time and preparation needed to make a team really work. At his best on the ovals, Brayton qualified fourth at Milwaukee and New Hampshire last year and scored a career-best third place at New Hampshire.

| Scott BRAYTON | |
|---|---|
| **Born:** 20-2-59, Coldwater, Michigan | |
| **Ht:** 5'9", **Wt:** 155 | |
| **Residence:** Coldwater, Michigan | |
| **Rookie Indy car season:** 1981 | |
| **Best Indy car finish:** 3rd (pre-1993) | |
| **Indy car poles:** 0 | |
| **Indy car earnings:** $3,594,596 | |

# Robbie **BUHL**

A native of Detroit, Michigan, Buhl raced Formula Ford in England as well as Sports Renault and Formula Atlantic in the United States before winning the 1989 Barber Saab series. Robbie moved to the Indy Lights (the support series of the PPG series) in 1990 and won his first race the following season. Last year he recorded 11 consecutive top three finishes and another win to claim the 1992 Indy Lights title. During the off season, he signed to drive for Dale Coyne Racing in the 1993 Indy car series.

Buhl's great, great grandfather and great, great uncle were mayors of Detroit in the 1880s, and Robbie is a national spokesman for the "Racing for Kids" charities, visiting thousands of sick kids at children's hospitals wherever he races. He is versatile in his leisure pursuits, spending any spare time playing ice hockey and driving snow mobiles, dirt bikes and off-road vehicles.

| Robbie BUHL | |
| --- | --- |
| Born: 2-9-65, Detroit, Michigan | |
| Ht: 5'9", Wt: 150 | |
| Residence: Detroit, Michigan | |
| Rookie Indy car season: 1993 | |
| Indy car poles: 0 | |

# Eddie **CHEEVER**

After Mario Andretti refocused on Indy cars in the early 1980s, Cheever was the only American racing in Formula One with regularity. A native of Phoenix, Arizona, Cheever was raised in Rome after his family moved there in connection with their fitness industry business.

Cheever began racing go-karts and won the Italian and European karting titles before graduating to Formula Fords at 16. After a meteoric rise through Formula Three and Formula Two, Eddie started his first Formula One race in 1976 with the Osella team and later drove for Tyrrell, Ligier, Renault, Alfa Romeo and Arrows.

Despite being a veteran of 133 Grands Prix, and finishing second on a number of occasions, a win eluded him and he moved to Indy car racing in 1990 with Chip Ganassi Racing, where he was named CART Rookie of the Year. As in Formula One, however, outright victory eluded him in the ensuing seasons and, after being released by Ganassi at the end of 1992, he signed to drive for the struggling Turley Motorsports team this season. Eddie's younger brother – Ross – is a successful F-3000 driver in Japan.

| Eddie CHEEVER | |
| --- | --- |
| Born: 10-1-58, Phoenix, Arizona | |
| Ht: 5'10", Wt: 150 | |
| Residence: Aspen, Colorado | |
| Rookie Indy car season: 1990 (One start in 1986) | |
| Best Indy car finish: 2nd (pre-1993) | |
| Indy car earnings: $2,480,907 | |

# Adrian **FERNANDEZ**

A native of Mexico City, Fernandez began racing motocross at the age of eight and competed in Formula Vee and Formula Ford in Mexico before moving to Europe in 1987 where he raced in the Benelux Formula Ford championship. He raced in England the following two seasons and finished eighth in the ESSO Formula Ford championship, before returning to Mexico where he won the Formula Three 1991 championship. Adrian moved to Indy Lights last year and was named Rookie of the Year on the strength of four wins and seven poles, and signed with Galles Racing to test and race Indy cars in 1993.

76

| Adrian FERNANDEZ | |
| --- | --- |
| Born: 20-4-65, Mexico City, Mexico | |
| Ht: 5'8", Wt: 150 | |
| Residence: Albuquerque, New Mexico | |
| Rookie Indy car season: 1993 | |

# Robby **GORDON**

Talented, precocious and brash, the Californian has been a breath of fresh air in Indy car racing since his debut with Ganassi Racing in 1992. He started motocross racing at seven and quickly graduated to off-road racing in the California desert, where he won his first event at 16. After winning numerous off-road titles, Robby signed with the prestigious Roush Racing sedan racing team in 1990 and immediately won GTO class in 24 Hours of Daytona. He went on to finish second in the 1990 GTO championship and score three more class wins at Daytona. After an impressive first season with Ganassi, in which he scored a couple of top-ten finishes and led the Cleveland race, he signed with AJ Foyt for 1993 and immediately helped that team return to prominence.

When he's not racing Indy cars Robby likes to go water- and snow-skiing.

| Robby GORDON | |
| --- | --- |
| Born: 2-1-69, Los Angeles, California | |
| Ht: 5'10", Wt: 160 | |
| Residence: Orange, California | |
| Rookie Indy car season: 1992 | |
| Best Indy car finish: 8th (pre-1993) | |
| Indy car earnings: $183,176 | |

# CONTENDERS
## Mike **GROFF**

After years of paying his dues, the 32-year-old Californian's efforts were finally rewarded last winter when he signed on as number two driver on three-time PPG champion Bobby Rahal's Rahal/Hogan team. Groff got his start driving on the dirt tracks of Southern California and was named Rookie of the Year at famed Ascot Park in 1981. Mike spent several years in Super Vee and the American Racing Series, winning both a Super Vee and ARS race at Milwaukee on one weekend in 1986, and earning the ARS title in 1989. Groff moved up to Indy cars with the small, but enthusiastic, Euromotorsports team and quickly demonstrated promise. He signed on

with AJ Foyt in mid-1991 and promptly finished eighth in his first outing with the team.

Mike has varied interests from restoring Porsches and modern architecture, to cycling and a secret passion to be a pro baseball player!

| Mike GROFF | |
|---|---|
| **Born: 16-11-61, Van Nuys, California** | |
| **Ht: 6', Wt: 168** | |
| **Residence: Columbus, Ohio** | |
| **Rookie Indy car season: 1990** | |
| **Best Indy car finish: 7th (pre-1993)** | |
| **Indy car earnings: $936,681** | |

77

## Stefan **JOHANSSON**

Another Formula One refugee, the likeable Swede came to the rescue of Tony Bettenhausen Racing last year after the team's disastrous Indianapolis 500. Two weeks after Bettenhausen failed to qualify for Indy, he decided to give Johansson a try-out in the Detroit race. Stefan, who won the 1980 British F-3 championship over the likes of Roberto Guerrero and Nigel Mansell, responded by qualifying eighth and finishing third and went on to earn CART Rookie of the Year honours. Detroit also gave Tony Bettenhausen his first visit to the podium as owner. With a third also at the Molson Indy Vancouver, Stefan notched up five finishes in the top 10.

A resident of Monte Carlo, Johansson drove a variety of F-1 teams, including Ferrari and McLaren, from 1982 through to 1991, finishing fifth in the World Driving Championship for

Ferrari in 1986. He cites Niki Lauda as his racing hero.

| Stefan JOHANSSON | |
|---|---|
| **Born: 8-9-56, Vaxjo, Sweden** | |
| **Ht: 5'8", Wt: 150** | |
| **Residence: Monte Carlo, Monaco** | |
| **Rookie Indy car season: 1992** | |
| **Best Indy car finish: 3rd (pre-1993)** | |
| **Indy car earnings: $377,122** | |

# Scott **PRUETT**

A former world go-karting champion, Pruett was one of the most successful sedan drivers in America in the 1980s, winning both the IMSA GTO and SCCA Trans-Am titles. He invested his entire life savings in renting a ride with Dick Simon Racing in the 1988 Long Beach Indy car race and was subsequently named to replace Bobby Rahal at Truesports Racing in 1989, when the two-time Indy car champ left the team. Scott led the Detroit Indy car race before finishing second to Emerson Fittipaldi, and went on to win Indy 500 and CART Rookie of the Year honours, but suffered horrendous injuries while testing with Truesports in the off-season.

Scott missed the entire 1990 season recouperating from his broken ankle, heels, knees and back, but returned to Indy cars in 1991 with Truesports' own chassis and scored five top five finishes. 1992 proved to be a disastrous season for Pruett, as Truesports announced it would cease operations at the end of the season and the team effort slowly deteriorated, leaving Scott without a full-time ride for 1993. He signed to drive a limited schedule with the fledgling Pro-Formance team, however, and immediately scored two top-ten finishes with ageing equipment.

| Scott PRUETT | |
| --- | --- |
| Born: 24-3-60, Sacramento, California | |
| Ht: 5'8", Wt: 150 | |
| Residence: Lake Tahoe, Nevada | |
| Rookie Indy car season: 1988 | |
| Best Indy car finish: 2nd (pre-1993) | |
| Indy car earnings: $2,166,691 | |

# Willy T **RIBBS**

B orn the son of a plumber in San Jose, California, Ribbs paid his way to England in 1977 and won six times in 11 races in the Star of Tomorrow Formula Ford championship. Ribbs made the most of irregular chances in the following years, for example outqualifying Michael Andretti and Al Unser Jr in front of the Formula One audience at the US Grand Prix Formula Atlantic race in 1982. However, he never had a full-time ride until he accepted an offer to race in the Trans-Am sedan series in 1983. Over the next few years he was a dominant performer, winning 22 races, before moving to IMSA sports cars where he was Driver of the Year in 1988 and '89.

Ribbs moved to Indy car racing in 1990 with the help of actor Bill Cosby

and the Raynor/Cosby team, then moved to the Derrick Walker team in '91 and became the first African-American to qualify for the Indianapolis 500. Lack of sponsorship limited him to one race in 1992, but Willy put a deal together this spring with Service Merchandise stores, Cosby and Walker for the balance of the 1993 and '94 seasons.

| Willy T. RIBBS | |
| --- | --- |
| Born: 3-1-56, San Jose, California | |
| Ht: 5'10", Wt: 165 | |
| Residence: San Jose, California | |
| Rookie Indy car season: 1990 | |
| Best Indy car finish: 6th (pre-1993) | |
| Indy car earnings: $544,299 | |

# Mark **SMITH**

The son of aviation entrepreneur Del Smith, Mark raced go-karts and Formula Fords before moving to Formula Super Vee in 1987. He raced on a two-car Super Vee team with his brother Mike (who gave up racing to fly jets).

Mark won the US Super Vee title in 1989 and moved to the Indy Lights series in 1990, when he was named Rookie of the Year. He won three races in Indy Lights in 1991 and '92, joined the rejuvenated Arciero Indy car team in 1993 and immediately showed an impressive combination of speed and maturity.

| Mark SMITH | |
| --- | --- |
| **Born:** 10-4-67, Portland, Oregon | |
| **Ht:** 5'10", **Wt:** 155 | |
| **Residence:** McMinnville, Oregon | |
| **Rookie Indy car season:** 1993 | |

# Jimmy **VASSER**

Another able young Californian, Vasser is a former national quarter midget and Formula Ford champion. He dominated the 1991 Toyota Atlantic series with six wins and eight pole positions, but failed to win the championship owing to repeated mechanical failures. Vasser signed to drive Indy cars in 1992 and had an impressive Indianapolis, setting a record that still stands as the fastest rookie qualifier (222.312 mph), but suffered a broken leg in a race day crash. After a lengthy recovery, Vasser finally returned to form in the latter stages of the season and jumped to prominence this year with a third place at Phoenix.

| Jimmy VASSER | |
| --- | --- |
| **Born:** 20-11-65, Canoga Park, California | |
| **Ht:** 5'9", **Wt:** 150 | |
| **Residence:** Discovery Bay, California | |
| **Rookie Indy car season:** 1992 | |
| **Best Indy car finish:** 7th (pre-1993) | |
| **Indy car earnings:** $313,325 | |

# Lyn **ST JAMES**

St James became the second woman to start the Indianapolis 500 after she qualified for the 1992 race at a speed of 220.150 mph; she went on to win Rookie of the Year honours with a seasoned drive to eleventh place. A veteran sedan racer, St James established 13 national and international speed records for women, including a then closed course record of 204.230 at Talladega International Speedway in 1985. She went on to co-drive the winning GTO entry in the 1987 and 1990 Daytona 24 Hour races, as well as the 1990 12 Hours of Sebring. St James also scored three top-five finishes in the 1990 Trans-Am series before passing her Indy car rookie test with Dick Simon Racing, a test that led to her joining Simon's team for the 1992 Indy 500.

Lyn is a television commentator with the ESPN network, and is also president of the Women's Sports Foundation and director of consumer affairs for the National Car Care Council.

| Lyn ST JAMES | |
| --- | --- |
| **Born:** 13-3-47 Willoughby, Ohio | |
| **Ht:** 5'6", **Wt:** 125 | |
| **Residence:** Daytona Beach, Florida | |
| **First Indy Car Race:** 1992 Indianapolis 500 | |
| **Best Finish:** 11th, 1992 Indy 500 | |
| **Indy car earnings** $187,953 | |

The 1993 PPG Indy Car World Series began with a question on everybody's mind: how would 1992 World Champion Nigel Mansell adapt to Indy car racing?

The first reigning World Champion to go Indy car racing, Mansell would be under intense scrutiny by those who see Indy car as nothing but a glorified national championship AND by those who believe the soul of Formula One has been co-opted by financial and technical forces. The answer was not long in coming.

### MANSELL LAPS IT UP

Mansell won his Indy car debut in grand style, only to crash heavily in his first oval racing weekend. But if his first two encounters with Indy car racing amounted to something of a draw, it wasn't long before Nigel established himself as an irresistible force in Indy car racing (see pp 82-83).

With Mario Andretti coming through to an enormously popular win at Phoenix and setting an Indy car closed course record in qualifying at MIS, it was quite a season for Newman/Haas Racing. Mansell won four of five oval starts, took another five podium finishes and became the first man to hold both the World Driving and PPG Championships simultaneously, albeit briefly.

In reality, Mansell was the only Lola driver to challenge the Penske PC22

Chevies of Fittipaldi (No.4 winning Indy 500 above) and Paul Tracy on a regular basis.

### FITTIPALDI FIGHTS BACK

Fittipaldi came through to win his second Indy 500 and Chevy's sixth straight against overwhelming odds favouring the Ford contingent. That, coupled with wins at Portland, Mid-Ohio and a host of other top finishes saw the Brazilian emerge at the biggest threat to Mansell's title hopes.

In fact, only a sub-par August

stopped Fittipaldi from taking a stranglehold on the PPG championship and, though he scored a timely win at Mid-Ohio to keep late pressure on Mansell, he was forced to settle for second overall.

### THE PAUL'N'RAUL ROADSHOW

For his part, Paul Tracy emerged as the fastest driver of the season. But while he won impressively at Long Beach, Toronto and Road America, unforced errors at Phoenix, Milwaukee and Mid-Ohio cost him three sure wins and any chance at the title.

In contrast, Raul Boesel was the year's most consistent driver. He gained a series of early second places at Phoenix, Milwaukee and Detroit, with consistent finishes in the points elsewhere, to keep his Duracell/Sadia Lola/Ford in title contention much of the year. The moral victor at Indianapolis, Boesel couldn't quite break through into the win column, but his 1993 season with the tightly budget Simon team was a resounding success nonetheless.

### THE UPS & DOWNS OF A SEE-SAW SEASON

Galles Racing had a turbulent, see-saw season. After spending the first third of the year in limbo, Danny Sullivan and Al Unser Jr waged a spirited battle for the win at Detroit that went to Sullivan, while Unser scored a masterly tactical victory at Vancouver. Neither played a prominent role in the championship, however. And while he didn't win a race, Robby Gordon was nothing short of sensational in bringing the A J Foyt Enterprises car to the podium for the first time since 1982.

Then there was Rahal/Hogan Racing. Although Bobby Rahal scored a fine second place with the Rahal/Hogan Chevy at Long Beach, the car was utterly uncompetitive at Indianapolis, and the defending PPG champion failed to qualify for the most important race of the year. In a Lola from Milwaukee onward, Rahal never quite overcame the five month head start he'd lost to the competition.

Meanwhile, Chip Ganassi Racing and Hall/VDS Racing wrote different chapters in frustration. The former

came within 2.5 seconds of sweeping the Indy 500 after Luyendyk's late run captured the pole and the Dutchman just failed to catch Fittipaldi for the win. Apart from a third place at Michigan, however, the Target Lola was often bogged down in the bottom third of the field. Teo Fabi was more consistent in the Pennzoil Lola, never getting near the podium – nor near the tail end. Mediocre is a word that comes to mind when describing Hall/VDS' season.

Likewise, Budweiser/King, Walker Motorsports and Tony Bettenhausen Motorsports had little to celebrate. Competitive on the short ovals, the Budweiser Lola-Chevy was off the pace on the road circuits and popular Roberto Guerrero was sacked after Vancouver. Scott Goodyear was quick at the beginning and the end of the season, but the Walker Lola-Ford was off the

pace through much of June, July and August. Stefan Johansson was often quick in Bettenhausen's Amax Penske PC22-Chevy, but reliability problems kept him off the podium until Vancouver.

## BEST OF THE REST
F-3000 graduate Andrea Montermini was nothing short of sensational in the Euromotorsports Lola-Chevy at Detroit, while Mark Smith put up several impressive performances in qualifying, only to be let down by mechanical problems on raceday. And Jimmy Vasser's third place at Phoenix was ample reward for a season of hard work in a year-old chassis.

Thus 1993 was in many ways a typical season of Indy car racing: no fewer than 14 different drivers on the podium and a championship decided in the penultimate race of the year.

# THE MANSELL CHALLENGE

Nigel Mansell is not the first World Champion to test the Indy car tracks. After all, Jack Brabham introduced the rear-engined car to Indianapolis; Jimmy Clark and Graham Hill both won the Indianapolis 500; Dennis Hulme and Jochen Rindt were no strangers to the Brickyard and, of course, Mario Andretti raced Indy cars long before (and after) winning the 1978 World Championship. And Emerson Fittipaldi won both the PPG title and the Indianapolis 500 in 1989.

But Mansell would be the first *reigning* World Champion to combat the Indy car circuits full time. And the very fact that he would be belted into the cockpit of a Lola T9300-Ford/Cosworth – rather than a Williams FW15C Renault – signalled a sea change in the way the world viewed Indy car racing. And the way Indy car racing viewed itself.

while he'd won his title in the all-conquering Williams FW14 Renault, there could be no doubting his talent, bravery and dedication to winning. Would Mansell make a shambles of Indy car racing, revealing that the emperors of American open wheel racing had no clothes? Or would he be at sea in an arena where no driver long enjoys a significant technological advantage, and where ovals, speedways and street circuits make up 75% of the schedule?

As is usually the case, the answer lay somewhere between the extremes. Although he won the PPG title race in magnificent fashion, he certainly didn't dominate the series. Where he'd won no fewer than nine F-1 races in 1992, including five in a row at one point, Nigel won just five Indy car races and went to the final two events with the title in doubt.

Mansell (and the F-1 world) also learned the hard way there's more to oval track racing than meets the eye. Fast in testing, even faster in practice for the Phoenix 200, Mansell got greedy and paid a heavy price. There are no gravel pits at Phoenix International Raceway.

Moreover, an argument could be made that he wasn't facing the sternest of opposition in 1993. Both Rick Mears and Michael Andretti were absent (Mears having retired and Andretti having gone off to test the F-1 waters with McLaren). Paul Tracy was still maturing and the Rahal/Hogan, Galles,

## ATLANTIC CROSSINGS

Indy car racing became something of a haven for disenchanted Formula One drivers in the 1980s, with men like Fittipaldi, Teo Fabi, Derek Daly, Roberto Guerrero, Bruno Giacomelli, Mike Thackwell, Jan Lammers, Raul Boesel, Kenneth Acheson, Rupert Kegan and others "crossing the pond". Some, like Fittipaldi and Fabi experienced tremendous success; others, like

Thackwell and Giacomelli, did not.

Inevitably, perhaps, when an ex-F1 driver was successful, the Formula One experts tended to write off Indy car racing as a second-rate series for "has beens." And whenever an ex-F1 driver failed, well he hadn't been rated in F1 anyway, had he?

## BREAKING IN ... AND BREAKING RECORDS

But with Mansell there could be no equivocating. Here was a World Champion at the top of his game, and

Ganassi, Walker, Bettenhausen, Hall/VDS and Budweiser/King teams had disappointing seasons for a score of reasons. Arguably, the only over-achievers were Raul Boesel and Robby Gordon, who both made the most of tightly financed operations.

## REBOUNDING TO VICTORY

And yet, there is no overstating Mansell's achievements in 1993.

He rebounded from his Phoenix accident with a useful third at Long Beach, then astounded his critics by not only qualifying easily at Indianapolis, with not a single lap of oval track racing to his credit, but nearly winning the race too. He led the Indianapolis 500 before former winners Emerson Fittipaldi and Arie Luyendyk outfoxed him on a late restart.

He rebounded from THAT lesson in Indy car racing to win on the historic Milwaukee Mile, as tough and demanding an oval as you'll find, and later won at fearsome Michigan International Speedway (MIS). He went on from there to beat Fittipaldi and Tracy in a no-holds-barred, *mano y mano y mano* battle at New Hampshire, amidst the swirling eddies of turbulent air, lapped traffic, pit stops, cautions and restarts that are the essence of oval track racing.

If it's true he enjoyed a significant advantage at MIS in the form of a development Ford/Cosworth XB engine, it's equally true he was at a disadvantage on the road and street circuits where the Penske PC22-Chevy package clearly outclassed his – or any other – Lola T9300-Ford/Cosworth. Moreover, owing to the nature of

street circuits, he was running on the Surfers Paradise, Detroit, Toronto, Cleveland, Vancouver and the revamped Long Beach street circuits for the first time.

## SIGNPOSTS AHEAD

And so the ultimate winners in 1993 were both Mansell and Indy car racing. Mansell learned much and showed just what a determined, talented man he is. Indy car racing got to showcase its tremendously exciting "product" to a whole new audience and, with Mansell set for a return, Michael Andretti back from F-1 and Al Unser Jr and Bobby Rahal back in fully competitive equipment, 1994 should be even better.

*Mansell with engineer Peter Gibbons (below, left) quickly established a superb working relationship.*

83

# SURFERS PARADISE, QUEENSLAND, MARCH 21st

## TRACK PROFILE

Born out of controversy, the Gold Coast Grand Prix at Surfers Paradise is surely one of the favourite stops on the Indy car calendar, despite the 24-hour plane trip and monumental logistical problems inherent in shipping some 36 Indy cars halfway round the world. Championship Auto Racing Teams was first approached by the race organizers about holding an Indy car race on Australia's Gold Coast in 1989.

When an agreement was finally reached and the race included on the 1991 schedule, open hostilities broke out between Indy's governing body and FISA (Federation Internationale de Sport Automobile), the world's recognized autosport governing body. Officials intending to work for the Gold Coast Grand Prix were threatened with having their licences permanently revoked; similar draconian threats were also made on any driver who participated in the race.

Championship Auto Racing Teams agreed to join ACCUS – FISA's US arm

– only to have FISA again refuse to grant a licence to the race. The race went off anyway and was generally rated a success, albeit a costly one as the Queensland government had to underwrite the race to the tune of $14 million. As the race was viewed as a big promotional event for tourism, this wasn't an immediate problem, but subsequent losses have placed the race's long term future in doubt.

Although the circuit is comprised of a rather uninspired collection of long straightaways and tight chicanes and corners, the facility is unquestionably the finest temporary circuit on the PPG Cup Series schedule in terms of amenities. The enclosed pit boxes, landscaped chicanes and a grassy, park-like paddock are all favourites among the Indy car drivers and teams, and the hospitality of the organizers, fans and local businesses is second to none.

The Gold Coast Grand Prix certainly has provided lots of entertainment in its short history. The inaugural event saw John Andretti come

through to win in his debut for the new Hall/VDS team after a combination of the blinding late afternoon sun and an accident involving two slower cars forced Rick Mears to take to an escape road late in the race.

Mears was leading again in 1992 after a torrential shower forced everyone to pit for rain tyres, but his team-mate Emerson Fittipaldi passed him, then bounced over a chicane, on the way to one of his most dramatic wins as an Indy car driver.

## TRACK FACTS

| | |
|---|---|
| ● Type of circuit: | temporary road course |
| ● Length: | 2.795 miles |
| ● Laps: | 65 |
| ● Distance driven: | 181.675 miles |
| ● No. of turns: | 16 |

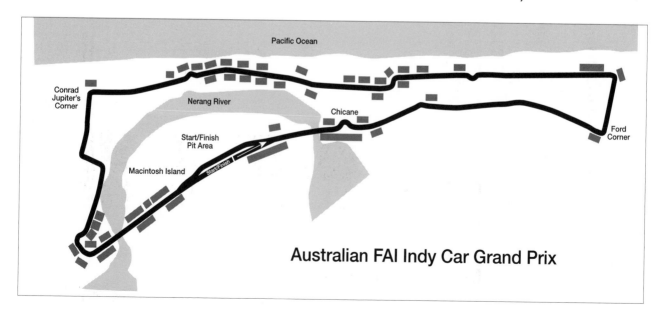

Australian FAI Indy Car Grand Prix

# RACE REPORT

Nigel Mansell made a hugely successful Indy car racing debut, winning his first race for Newman/Haas Racing from pole after an entertaining duel with Emerson Fittipaldi's Marlboro Penske. There was nothing easy about Mansell's first Indy car win, however.

First, Nigel was comprehensively blown away by Fittipaldi, Penske team-mate Paul Tracy and young sensation Robby Gordon on the opening lap. Then, after clawing his way back to the front and passing Fittipaldi for the lead in a cloud of tyre smoke, Mansell was assessed a stop 'n' go pit stop penalty for passing the Brazilian under a yellow (or caution) flag situation. However, the penalty was not as severe as it

might have been as the Newman/Haas crew was able to change tyres and refuel Mansell's Kmart/ Texaco Lola during the penalty pit stop. So he lost comparatively little time in the process.

With Tracy falling out with mechanical problems and Fittipaldi forced to slow his pace owing to poor fuel mileage readings (incorrect readings, as it turned out), Mansell was able to pull away to a victory that proved enormously popular among the local fans.

"I'm just delighted with what I've done," said Mansell. "This is just brilliant. It's my first win in Australia and Australia is like a home country for me. It's the closest thing to England ... I think it's been a fantastic race ... I can't remember the last time I had this much

fun. It was good, clean, hard racing."

Gordon made a big impression by coming home third in his debut with A J Foyt Enterprises, while Mario Andretti could do no better than fourth after mysteriously losing a nose wing from his car at mid-race. Arie Luyendyk had a good race in his first outing with Chip Ganassi Racing and came home fifth, the final driver on the lead lap, while defending PPG champion Bobby Rahal managed to hold off Eddie Cheever for sixth place. Raul Boesel, Teo Fabi, Scott Goodyear, Hiro Matsushita and Stefan Johansson rounded out the points-getters in CART's first-through-to-twelfth scoring system.

*Off on the right foot*: Mansell earned the pole and won the race in his Indy car debut.

# PHOENIX, ARIZONA, APRIL 4th

## TRACK FACTS

| | |
|---|---|
| ● *Type of circuit:* | oval |
| ● *Length:* | 1 miles |
| ● *Laps:* | 200 |
| ● *Distance driven:* | 200 miles |
| ● *No. of turns:* | 4:1&2 banked at 11°/3&4 at 9° |

## TRACK PROFILE

Situated in Arizona's Valley of the Sun, the city of Phoenix has hosted championship races dating back to 1905 and 1915. But it wasn't until 1950 that national championship events became a fixture in Phoenix with races on the one-mile dirt oval at the State Fairgrounds near the centre of town. Many of the sport's legendary names won on the notoriously rough Fairgrounds track, men like Bill Vukovich, Tony Bettenhausen and Arizona's own Jimmy Bryan.

Following the 1962 race, the Fairgrounds commission decided to stop racing by 1964. This enabled local enthusiast Richard Hogue to incorporate a modern mile oval into the road racing circuit he was already in the process of constructing 30 miles west of town, on the edge of the Santa Estrella mountains.

Thus was Phoenix International Raceway born and, appropriately, A J Foyt won the inaugural 100-mile event in 1964 by beating Roger McCluskey and Parnelli Jones. Over the years, PIR's unique layout, featuring steep banking in Turns One and Two, a "dogleg" midway down the backstretch and the wide, but nearly flat Turns Three and Four, has proved to be a stern test of drivers' oval track racing ability. Only the best have won at Phoenix – from Foyt and the Unsers to Mario Andretti and Michael Andretti, Johnny Rutherford, Gordon Johncock, Tom Sneva, Rick Mears and Bobby Rahal.

Situated in the Southwest desert, where a bad winter is better than the summers in most places, PIR is traditionally the sight of extensive pre-season testing, and each winter word spreads of the fantastic speeds achieved in testing at Phoenix. By the time the race is held in April, however, temperatures can be anywhere from the high 70s to over 100 degrees, and the off-season times are rarely duplicated when it counts. Still, the pre-

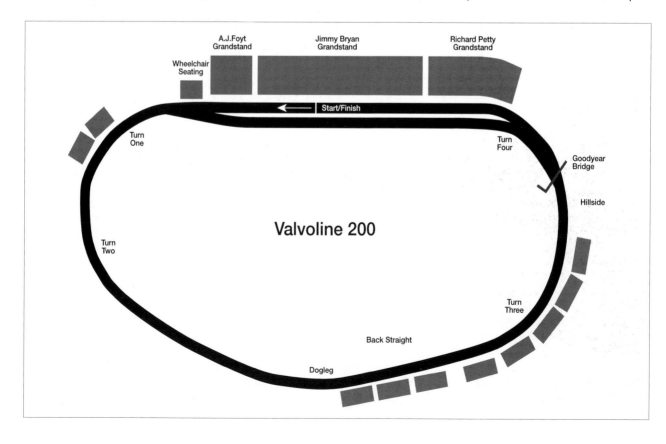

season testing psyche game is very much part and parcel of PIR.

The track has also been the site of some fearsome accidents, none more famous than Rutherford's crash in 1980, which saw his Chaparral flip upside down on exiting Turn Four and skid to a stop on its roll-over hoop in front of a stunned grandstand. Miraculously, "Lone Star JR" escaped with only minor bumps and bruises.

One of the most memorable races in Indy car history took place at PIR in 1987 when Roberto Guerrero – at that time the hard luck man of Indy car racing – scored his first win. Starting last, Roberto stormed through the field and took the lead on Lap 87, but was assessed as a stop'n'go penalty for running over an air hose in pit lane. Undaunted, he roared back to lap the entire field – except for second place finisher Bobby Rahal – and score a popular maiden Indy car win.

## RACE REPORT

▶ Mario Andretti scored his 52nd Indy car triumph in fortuitous fashion after the Penskes of Paul Tracy and Emerson Fittipaldi crashed in rapid succession in the closing stages of the Valvoline 200. Coupled with his wins in Formula One, sports car endurance racing, midgets, sprint, champ dirt and stock cars dating back to the late 1950s, the win gave Andretti 100 major victories in five decades.

Andretti's win also came as a welcome fillip for Newman/Haas Racing, which was reduced to a one car effort when Nigel Mansell crashed heavily the previous day (*see cover picture and page 2 caption*). In Mansell's absence, Scott Goodyear edged Andretti for pole ahead of Fittipaldi, Tracy and Roberto Guerrero. But once the race got underway, it was all Tracy

**"I'm the eternal optimist. I never give up. Never."**

*Winner Mario Andretti on scoring his 52nd Indy car win*

as the young Canadian took the lead on Lap 11 and simply drove into the distance. 31 laps later Tracy passed Fittipaldi a second time to put himself a full lap ahead of the field, and he later put his team-mate another lap down in the most dominating performance in an Indy car race in recent memory.

With less than 40 miles remaining, however, Tracy tried an ill-advised pass of the fifth placed Jimmy Vasser. When Vasser held his line, Tracy was squeezed down on the track and spun into the same wall that had welcomed Mansell with open arms little more than 24 hours before. That left Fittipaldi with a full lap lead on Andretti. When the race was restarted (following the removal of Tracy's car), Emerson promptly deposited his car in the Turn Three wall, the legacy of running over debris from his team-mate's car!

That left Mario with a full lap's advantage over Raul Boesel with Vasser now up to third ahead of Al Unser Jr, Teo Fabi and Arie Luyendyk. Having seen more than one race slip through

his fingers in recent years, Mario was not about to let this one get away, and so he cruised to his first win in the 1990s. And made no apologies for inheriting the victory:

"I'm as happy as I was with my first win," he said. "Today was one of those days – a lucky day. I thank the Man upstairs because I've had so many of these days where a race was taken away from me." But he added "I'm the eternal optimist. I never give up. Never."

Scott Pruett scored a welcome seventh for the underfunded Pro-Formance team ahead of Indy car debutante David Kudrave, while Mark Smith, Hiro Matsushita, Marco Greco and Ross Bentley rounded out the top twelve.

*Quick service*: Roberto Guerrero takes on 40 gallons of methanol and four tyres in the Phoenix pits.

# LONG BEACH, CALIFORNIA, APRIL 18th

## TRACK PROFILE

Once little more than a figment in the imagination of entrepreneur Chris Pook, the Long Beach Grand Prix sparked a worldwide growth in racing through the streets of major cities from Detroit to Birmingham.

Pook, a British emigré to Southern California, envisioned a street race as a major event that would help rejuvenate the moribund beach/port city of Long Beach, near neighbour to Los Angeles. He began drumming up support for the event in the early 1970s and, contrary to all expectations, managed to pull off a Formula 5000 race in downtown Long Beach in 1975 as a prelude to a Formula One race there the following spring.

The US Grand Prix West was a huge success, and ran from 1976 until 1984, when the sky-rocketing prices associated with running a Formula One race brought Pook and Championship Auto Racing Teams together. Long Beach has been an Indy car race ever

since, and before Danny Sullivan's win in 1992, either an Andretti or an Unser race every year.

Mario won the race in 1984, '85 and '87; Michael Andretti scored his maiden Indy car win at Long Beach in 1986 and then Al Unser Jr won four in a row from 1988 to 1991.

Indeed, Unser was on his way to a fifth win when Sullivan – his erstwhile team-mate – inadvertently knocked him out of the lead in the closing stages of the 1992 race.

### TRACK FACTS

- **Type of circuit:** temporary road course
- **Length:** 1.59 miles
- **Laps:** 105
- **Distance driven:** 166.95 miles
- **No. of turns:** 9

## RACE REPORT

▶ Paul Tracy atoned for his Phoenix gaffe with a superbly judged win through the streets of Long Beach. Coming back from not one but two unscheduled pit stops for cut tyres, Tracy outlasted Rahal and Mansell in one of the most contentious Indy car races in years. All told, CART officials dished out more than $20,000 in fines for rough driving and un-sportsmanlike conduct, and placed three drivers (Eddie Cheever, Robby Gordon and Arie Luyendyk) on probation.

Qualifying saw Mansell earn his second Indy car pole, despite back pains stemming from his encounter with the Phoenix Raceway wall a fortnight before. Once again, however, his hard-won advantage evaporated at the drop of the green flag as Tracy surged by the

**88**

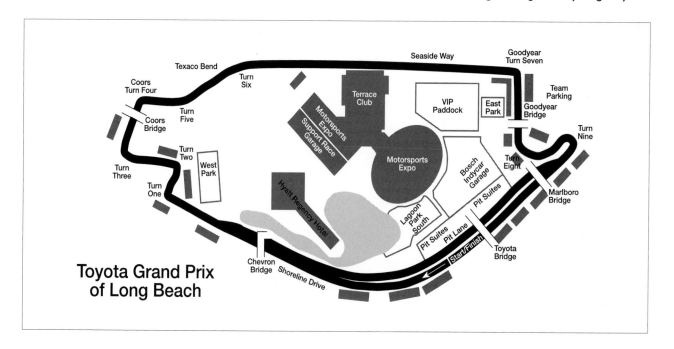

## Toyota Grand Prix of Long Beach

Kmart/Havoline Lola on the run to Turn One with Scott Goodyear and Mario Andretti in hot pursuit.

Tracy seemingly had the race under control as Al Unser Jr – a four time Long Beach winner – moved up and began harrying Mansell. The two diced before tangling in the close confines of Turn Two, with a mightily upset Unser retiring on the spot.

"I've never seen anybody block me as bad as Nigel blocked me today," he said. "He parked me against the wall. What goes around comes around."

Surprisingly, Mansell found himself in the lead after Tracy made an extra stop to replace a flat tyre and Goodyear was penalized for exceeding the 70 mph speed limit on pit lane. But when the race went under a lengthy caution to remove the cars of Gordon and Cheever (after Gordon had, by all accounts, intentionally driven into the side of Cheever's machine), it was

**❝I've never seen anybody block me as bad as Nigel blocked me today. He parked me against the wall. What goes around comes around.❞**

*Al Unser Jr on his tussle with Mansell.*

Tracy – whose earlier unplanned pit stop now gave him sufficient fuel to make the finish – in the lead.

Suffering from the loss of second gear, Mansell fell to sixth behind Tracy, Raul Boesel, the surging cars of Rahal and Goodyear and Mario Andretti. But Mario and Raul fell out in rapid order with mechanical problems and Goodyear smacked the wall exiting the Turn Nine hairpin, and so Tracy came home to his first Indy car win from Rahal and Mansell.

"Deep down I knew that I was capable," said Tracy, "but things just slipped away. I tried harder and harder and just made mistakes. It's good to get

the monkey off our backs. This is something to build on."

Teo Fabi and Roberto Guerrero finished ahead of young Robbie Buhl who gave Dale Coyne Racing its best ever finish with a sixth place, while Scott Pruett scored his second consecutive seventh ahead of Danny Sullivan, Cheever, Mark Smith and Arie Luyendyk – the latter two having indulged in a barging match on the final lap – while Boesel was credited with twelfth place.

**Frustration in the streets**: Fittipaldi was slowed by a leaky turbocharger at Long Beach.

89

# INDIANAPOLIS MOTOR SPEEDWAY, INDIANA, MAY 30th

## TRACK PROFILE

The epicentre of Indy car racing is located at the corner of 16th Street and Georgetown Road in the Indianapolis suburb of Speedway: the Indianapolis Motor Speedway.

Not just the most important race of the year in Indy car racing, the Indianapolis 500 is the world's largest single-day sporting event with a crowd in excess of 400,000 people.

The Indianapolis 500 is a month-long event, with practice from 11 am to 6 pm each day for a week before the first weekend of qualifying; another week of practice leads to the second weekend of qualifying before the race is held on the final Sunday of the month of May (Memorial/Decoration Day, a US Public Holiday).

A car's starting position is

### TRACK FACTS

| | |
|---|---|
| ● Type of circuit: | superspeedway |
| ● Length: | 2.5 miles |
| ● Laps: | 200 |
| ● Distance driven: | 500 miles |
| ● No. of turns: | 4: banked at 9° |

determined not only by how fast it qualifies, but when. Only cars qualifying on the first Saturday are eligible for pole position; thereafter, cars line up by speed based on which day they qualify. Therefore, as sometimes happens, a car may qualify faster than the pole sitter yet start deep in the pack because its

qualifying run came on the second weekend!

Built in 1909 as an automotive proving ground and race track, the Indianapolis Motor Speedway was originally paved with a mixture of crushed stone and tar. After a number of serious accidents in initial events, the management undertook a massive repaving project and when the inaugural Indy 500 was run in 1911, the track boasted a surface made of more than 3.2 million bricks – hence the Speedway's popular nickname, "the Brickyard".

Except for interruptions for World War I and II, the Indianapolis 500 has been run every year since 1911. A group headed by World War I flying ace Eddie Rickenbacker purchased the facility from the original owners in

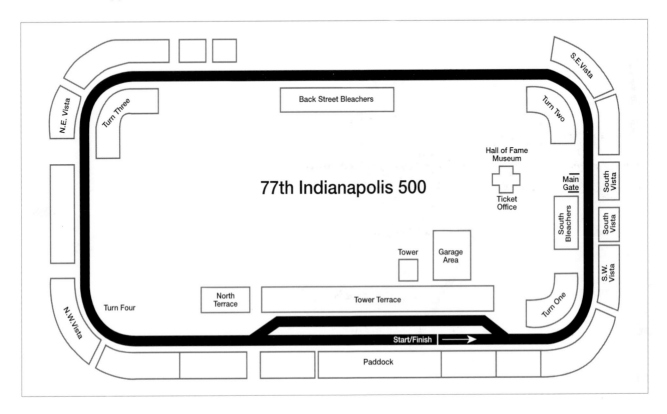

77th Indianapolis 500

1927, then Tony Hulman acquired the Speedway in 1945.

When Hulman took possession, the Speedway was in drastic need of repair, having lain fallow since the spring of 1941. Hulman launched a long-term improvement programme, initially replacing the old wooden grandstands with steel and concrete structures, then building a new race control tower, pits and pit grandstands. All new grandstands were gradually added during the 1950s and '60s; corporate hospitality suites came next and then the multimillion dollar IMS museum and executive office building was added in 1976. On-going improvements to the facility have continued, with new grandstands being added as recently as the winter of '92, bringing the seating capacity to more than 300,000. The infield, which contains several holes of a championship golf course, serves as a

*Object of desire: Displayed on pit lane throughout the month of May, the Borg Warner trophy is the object of curiosity for the throngs that flock to the Speedway daily, and of desire for the 33 drivers who "make the show" by qualifying for a pit lane appearance (below).*

giant parking lot and home to another 100,000 or so fans on race and qualifying days.

Measuring 2.5 miles in length, the Indianapolis Motor Speedway features two 3,300 foot long straightaways, four turns each 1,220 feet in length and banked at 9 degrees, 12 minutes, and two 600-foot "short chutes" connecting the turns. Portions of the track were resurfaced with asphalt beginning in 1937 and the entire track was repaved in 1976 and again in 1989. However, a 36-inch section of the original brick surface still remains to mark the start/finish line.

Since Ray Harroun won the inaugural Indianapolis 500 in 1911 at an average speed of 74.602 mph, speeds have climbed almost continually. Peter De Paolo became the first man to average more than 100 mph for the 500 mile race in 1925, but it wasn't until Jim

Clark won the 1965 race in his Lotus-Ford that the race average topped 150 mph. The fastest Indy 500 race average goes to Arie Luyendyk, who won the 1990 race at a speed of 185.981.

A race that dates back more than 75 years has seen its fair share of triumph, drama and tragedy. Only three men – A J Foyt, Al Unser and Rick Mears – have won the race four times, and each was involved in a number of memorable races. Foyt, for example, duelled with Eddie Sachs for the final 200 miles of the 1961 race as they passed and repassed one another more than a dozen times. With 15 laps remaining Foyt was forced to pit for a final splash of fuel, seemingly handing the race to Sachs. But Sachs pitted with just four laps remaining to change a badly worn tyre, handing Foyt the first of his four wins. Sachs, one of the most popular drivers in the sport, would never win the Indy 500. Indeed, he would perish in a monumental first-lap accident in 1964 that also killed rookie driver Dave McDonald.

Unser had already won three Indy 500s in 1987 when he was called to replace the injured Danny Ongais on the Penske team well into the month of May. When the Penske PC16 chassis proved uncompetitive, Roger Penske resurrected year-old March 86Cs for Rick Mears and Danny Sullivan, then literally pulled a third March from the showroom floor of one of his auto dealerships for Unser. Al qualified 20th, narrowly avoided a multi-car crash on the first lap and steadily moved up through the field. This day belonged to Mario Andretti however; or so it seemed. Starting from pole, Mario led 170 of the first 177 laps, only to coast to a halt with a broken engine. Roberto Guerrero assumed the lead with Unser second, but a slipping clutch on his final pit stop dropped Roberto a lap behind Al who came through to lead the only 18 laps that truly counted.

In 14 years at Indianapolis, Rick Mears had never spun let alone crashed. But the day before qualifying began a

wheel came loose on his '91 Penske at over 230 mph. Rick slammed into the wall in Turn One and ground along for nearly ¼ mile before stopping. Although he escaped serious injury, the tender bones and tissue in his feet (which were grievously injured in a crash in Canada in 1984) were done a power of no-good by the impact. Later that day, though, after just six laps in his back-up car, Mears unleashed a mindboggling lap of more than 226 mph to set fastest time of the day. Two days later, he earned his sixth Indy 500 pole at a speed of 224.133 mph.

As in 1987 though, it appeared the race belonged to Andretti – Michael Andretti, that is. Michael led 96 of the first 183 laps, at one point nearly putting Mears a full lap in arrears. But Mears, a master at working to reach his car's optimum performance at the end of a race, battled back. Rick was leading with 16 laps remaining when Danny Sullivan's engine blew up, resulting in a full course caution to remove the stricken car from the track.

On the restart Rick and Michael ran side by side past the pits, accelerating to 230 mph as they entered Turn One. Mears held the inside but Andretti swooped to the outside in a breathtaking move that seemed destined to win the race. But Rick was unphased. He stayed with the leader through the following lap and, when Michael swung low into Turn One to start Lap 188 Mears powered around the outside, duplicating Andretti's breathtaking move of the previous lap, and going on to join Foyt and Unser as four-time Indy 500 champions.

# RACE REPORT

▶ Emerson Fittipaldi put all his considerable experience to good use, on two late restarts, to jump past Nigel Mansell and then hold off Arie Luyendyk to win his second Indianapolis 500. The win was Fittipaldi's third top three finish at Indy in the past five years, and marked Penske Racing's ninth Indy 500 win since first coming to the Brickyard in 1969.

*"Gentlemen, start your engines":* At 10:51 am the 33 drivers start their Indy cars engines and then follow the pace car for the rolling start at 11:00. The pace car (far right of picture in pit lane) is used to control the speed of race cars not only before the start, but also during caution periods once the race is underway.

Following the accident-strewn 1992 race, the Indianapolis Motor Speedway embarked on a major reconstruction project designed to limit speeds and lessen the severity of contact with the retaining walls. First, the wide aprons on the inside of the four corners were replaced by a "dedicated" warm-up lane separated from the racing surface by a strip of grass. Next, the inside edges of the turns were marked by irregular strips of pavement – rumble strips – to discourage drivers from purposely short-cutting the corners. Finally, the old retaining walls were replaced with higher, thicker versions.

The net effect of these changes was to alter the drivers' approach to the Speedway. In recent years, lapping the Speedway at full throttle had become commonplace. And it wasn't just the drivers with cars that handled perfectly; those with an understeering car could simply drive down to the apron in the turns knowing that as the car "pushed" out towards the wall on the exit, there was a cushion of track to work with. With the apron – and the cushion – gone, Indianapolis became a much more demanding track in terms of handling. Indeed, few – if any – drivers talked about lapping at full throttle.

"There is only one line," said 1992 Indy pole winner Roberto Guerrero. "The only way you can go fast is to have the car working perfectly. Before, you could adjust your driving to the conditions of the track."

The changes to the track, coupled with new rules that reduced the downforce on the cars themselves, also meant that the days of running two and three abreast were a thing of the past. There simply wasn't enough track to work with, especially given the fact that the new rules made the cars more susceptible than ever to aerodynamic turbulence.

With drivers cracking the throttle at least twice a lap – on the entry to Turns One and Three – the Buick powered cars which had been so competitive in years past found themselves at a disadvantage. With its narrow power band, the Buicks took too long to build up speed again after a major "lift".

The Ford/Cosworth XBs had no such problems and dominated the week of practice leading up to the first day of qualifying – with Arie Luyendyk, Mario Andretti, Scott Goodyear and Raul Boesel topping the daily speed charts with lap speeds in excess of 225 mph. The Chevy C-powered cars struggled to match the Fords in straightaway speeds, with the Penskes of Emerson Fittipaldi and

**94**

Paul Tracy barely able to edge over 224 mph and the rest happy to break 220. In an amazing comeback from the horrible leg and ankle injuries he suffered at Indy in 1992, Jeff Andretti led the Buick stable in the mid-222s.

And what of Nigel Mansell? Having required surgery to repair an internal lesion caused by his Phoenix accident, Nigel missed much of the first week of practice but sailed through his rookie tests and ran as fast as 224 mph as Pole Day loomed (so called because pole position is awarded to the fastest qualifier on the first of the four scheduled days of qualifying).

The first day of qualifying at Indianapolis is always special, as the tension is packed into five minute segments when each driver takes to the track, quite alone, under the gaze of his peers and ¼ million fans. Mario Andretti was among the first to qualify and he duly established a mark of 223.414 for the rest to shoot at – which they did most of the day without success. Luyendyk recorded a leisurely 215 lap and pulled off to try again; Goodyear and Boesel failed to better 222 and three time World Champion

Nelson Piquet capped his own comeback from injuries with a 217.949.

The cool of the afternoon found three men with a chance to bump Mario from pole: Luyendyk, Fittipaldi and Mansell. Arie took to the track in the Target/Scotch Video Lola with an hour remaining and nailed a four lap average of 223.967 to take his first Indy car pole (ironically, he'd won the first of his three Indy car victories at Indianapolis in 1990). Having practised at 222.9 in the heat of the day, Mansell

> **❝It's the first time I've raced on an oval – I'm not making any excuses, I just goofed up.❞**
>
> *Third place, Nigel Mansell*

took to the track with high hopes only to be disappointed with a 220.255 and when Fittipaldi could only manage a 220.150 after he had to switch to his spare car, the pole was Luyendyk's.

Bobby Rahal became the focus of attention over the next week as he struggled with his spare Rahal/Hogan-Chevy after posting a vulnerable 217.140 speed that first weekend. When he failed to reach competitive speeds he was "bumped" from the field by Eddie Cheever in the waning moments of the final day of qualifying. Rahal would not be the only surprise on the sidelines on race day, for A J Foyt had decided to announce his retirement from competition moments before qualifying began on Pole Day.

Following the customary pomp and circumstance that precedes the world's largest single-day sporting event, Boesel took advantage of his spot on the outside of the front row to outdrag Luyendyk and Mario into Turn One and lead the opening segment of the race. In that time a pattern was established, namely that with side-by-side running in the turns a dicey proposition at best, the only way to pass a car running at

similar speeds was to wait for that driver to make a mistake or get caught behind slower traffic.

Out in the lead, Boesel had free sailing until he began lapping slower cars as early as Lap Ten. Although he had perhaps the best handling car in the race, Raul's hopes of duplicating Luyendyk's 1990 feat of winning his first Indy car race at Indianapolis would be dashed by a couple of controversial penalties for passing cars on pit lane. For his part, Goodyear made an early pit stop to replace a suspected cut tyre and fell from contention, and Paul Tracy crashed while duelling with Scott Brayton. Luyendyk ran steadily in the top five while Fittipaldi moved into contention. But it was the Newman/Haas cars of Andretti and, surprisingly, Mansell, who dominated proceedings, with Andretti leading 70 of the first 172 laps before he too was assessed a stop 'n' go penalty on a marginal call.

Thus it was Mansell, of all people, who found himself leading the race from Fittipaldi and Luyendyk when Lyn St James brought out a full course yellow 18 laps from the finish. Not that these three were the only potential winners. Thanks to the tough passing conditions and low attrition rate (24 of 33 starters were still in the contest), no fewer than ten cars were on the lead lap with Boesel, Mario Andretti, Brayton, Goodyear, Al Unser Jr, Teo Fabi and John Andretti also in the hunt.

The restart on Lap 184 was a classic. As Mansell brought the field down for the green flag, Fittipaldi and Luyendyk accelerated as hard as they could. Fittipaldi fairly flew by Mansell as the trio whistled towards Turn One, and as Nigel went to the inside in an effort to hold on to second, Luyendyk did the impossible and drove around the outside of the KMart/Havoline machine in Turn One.

"I thought I got on the gas early

**"There is no Grand Prix that can compare to Indy . . . My second Indianapolis is better than my second (World) Championship. It's like a dream."**

*Winner Emerson Fittipaldi*

*Winning isn't everything: It's the only thing. Even the victory stand is reserved exclusively for the winner.*

enough," said Mansell. "I was going down the straight and all of a sudden all I see is *vroooom, vroooom* as Emerson and Arie went past. I just didn't execute it that good and I didn't get a good jump."

Trying hard to make up for his mistake, Mansell walloped the wall exiting Turn Two and, although his Lola remained miraculously intact, brought out another caution flag. This time it was Luyendyk's turn to try and outfox Fittipaldi, but the Brazilian would have none of it.

"Emerson slowed the field down to such a slow speed that I had to go back to second gear," explained Arie. "And he accelerated when his car was in a straight line and I was still running through Turn Three. When I accelerated, the car went sideways. I had to go up to third gear and by then he had the run on me."

Although the race was close – the top six finishers crossed the line covered by six seconds – there was never any doubt as to the outcome once Fittipaldi got the drop on Luyendyk, and the Brazilian came home a euphoric winner.

"This was the race of my life," he said. "There is no Grand Prix that can compare to Indy. To win the first time was fantastic, and to win the second we had to work very hard; it is something very special. My second Indianapolis is better than my second (World) Championship. It's like a dream."

As for Mansell, though frustrated in his efforts to become the first man to win his rookie Indy 500 since Graham Hill did the trick in 1966, he was a runaway winner in the Indy 500 Rookie of the Year balloting and had no complaints.

"The team did a fantastic job and what mistakes were made today were made by me," he said. "It's the first time I've raced on an oval. All the procedures are new to me. I'm not making any excuses, I just goofed up on a couple of them."

95

## ROUND 5

FULL RACE RESULTS – PAGES 120-123

# THE MILWAUKEE MILE, WEST ALLIS, WISCONSIN JUNE 6th

### TRACK FACTS

| | |
|---|---|
| ● *Type of circuit:* | oval |
| ● *Length:* | 1 mile |
| ● *Laps:* | 200 |
| ● *Distance driven:* | 200 miles |
| ● *No. of turns:* | 4: banked at 9° |

### TRACK PROFILE

This one-mile oval, set in the Wisconsin fairgrounds in a blue-collar neighbourhood of Milwaukee, is the only circuit on the Indy car schedule that can match the Indianapolis Motor Speedway for history. The Milwaukee Mile (as it is commonly known) has been holding races since 1904.

For its first 50 years, the Milwaukee Mile was a dirt track and winners there included some of the legendary names in American racing: Rex Mays, Wilbur Shaw, Tony Bettenhausen, for example.

Milwaukee also enjoyed other traditions. For openers, the Milwaukee race was held on the weekend following the Indianapolis 500 and so benefited from the enormous interest generated by the Memorial Day classic. And in most years, Milwaukee held not just one national championship race in early June, but a second race in August – a tradition that was discontinued in 1983 owing to pressures to expand the PPG Cup Series to additional venues.

Finally paved in 1954, the Milwaukee Mile has witnessed a number of historic races, not the least of which was Jimmy Clark's first Indy car win in the August race in 1964 – nearly a year before his more celebrated Indy 500 victory. One of the most memorable sights at Milwaukee came in 1965 when A J Foyt's rear-engined car wasn't ready in time for the race, so he took his upright roadster off the trailer and proceeded to qualify the out-dated car on the pole.

Milwaukee has gone through some lean stretches – indeed little money was put into maintenance or improvements at the facility in the 1970s and '80s. Ironically, the lack of improvements has contributed to the track's appeal, for the bumpy track surface has kept speeds in check and, in combination with the wide, flat turns, produced exciting racing.

When combined with intangibles such as the massive concrete grandstands fronting the pit straight and the row of neighbourhood houses a stone's throw away from the back straight, the close racing, history and atmosphere at Milwaukee make for one of the year's most enjoyable events.

In 1992 Carl Haas took over management and promotion for the facility, and quickly began making amends for the years of neglect. Dilapidated wooden grandstands were replaced with concrete and aluminium structures, new retaining walls were installed and parts of the facility received their first coat of paint in 20 years. Haas fully intends to bring the Milwaukee Mile up to first-class standards in the coming years – his challenge will be to do that while keeping Milwaukee's intangible atmosphere in place.

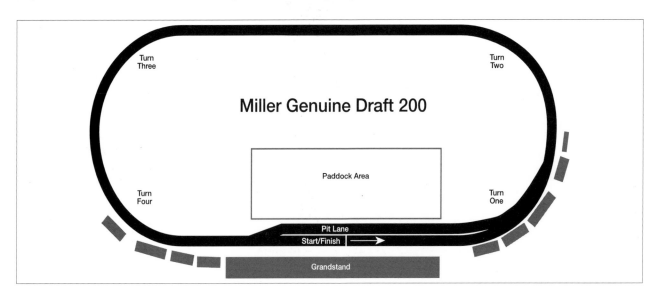

Turn Three

Turn Two

Miller Genuine Draft 200

Paddock Area

Turn Four

Turn One

Pit Lane

Start/Finish

Grandstand

# RACE REPORT

► The Milwaukee Indy car race can't help but be viewed in the context of the month-long (May) Indianapolis 500 that ends just five days before practice starts here. Often the team that wins Indy comes to Milwaukee with such momentum that they're nearly unstoppable. At other times the Indy 500 victors arrive here in such a fog – from all the personal appearances and celebrating – that they're never a factor.

This year, the one man who dominated the Indy 500 in spirit – if not the results – picked up where he left off at Milwaukee. Raul Boesel, moral victor at the Speedway, utterly demolished all comers in practice and qualifying and set a new track record of 21.719 seconds, more than half a second faster than Emerson Fittipaldi, with Scott Goodyear and Paul Tracy making an all-Canadian second row ahead of Mario Andretti and Scott Brayton. Nigel Mansell, making his first start on a mile oval, lined up seventh.

Although Boesel quickly established himself as the man to beat at the green flag, Goodyear came on strong to take the lead at the first round of pit stops. But the Mackenzie Lola faded on its second set of tyres, enabling Tracy to take over until he found himself in the wrong place at the wrong time and hit Arie Luyendyk while avoiding Adrian Fernandez's crash on Lap 141. With Goodyear falling out with a broken gearbox, the race boiled down to a duel between Raul and Nigel.

Raul had stopped for fuel and tyres during the caution to remove Goodyear from the track on Lap 115 and, thanks to the Tracy-Luyendyk-Fernandez shunt, could make it to the chequered flag without another stop. On the other hand, Mansell stopped for fuel and tyres on Lap 141 and fell behind Boesel. The KMart/Havoline Lola had fresher tyres however, and Nigel was able to track down Raul in the closing stages, finally passing the Duracell/Sadia Lola with 25 laps remaining. Although a late yellow/caution flag gave Boesel one final

chance to repass Mansell, the Brit had learned his lesson about restarts at Indianapolis and held off Raul's final bid for victory. "I learned a very painful lesson at Indianapolis on the restart," Mansell conceded. "I figured I'm not going to let that happen again. So I slowed down – I think Raul knew what I was doing – and then I just floored it and hoped it was enough."

Fittipaldi came home an unusually quiet third ahead of Bobby Rahal, who was having his first outing in a 1993 Lola after abandoning the Rahal/Hogan chassis in the wake of his failure to qualify for Indianapolis. The lot of them finished two laps free of Al Unser Jr, Brayton and Roberto Guerrero, while Jimmy Vasser underlined Simon Racing's increasingly formidable look with an eighth place (giving the team three top-ten spots) ahead of Teo Fabi, Robby Gordon, Willy T Ribbs and Olivier Grouillard, who was making his first Indy car start after just failing to qualify at Indy.

*Critics confounded: Mansell streaks to victory in just his second oval race.*

# BELLE ISLE PARK, DETROIT, MICHIGAN, JUNE 13th

| TRACK FACTS | |
|---|---|
| ● Type of circuit: | temporary road course |
| ● Length: | 2.1 miles |
| ● Laps: | 77 |
| ● Distance driven: | 161.7 miles |
| ● No. of turns: | 14 |

## TRACK PROFILE

Like Long Beach, the Detroit Indy car race began as an F-1 event when, with heavy subsidies from the American auto industry, the US Grand Prix was organized around the striking towers of the Renaissance Center in 1982.

The Detroit GP was always one of the least favourite races on the F-1 calendar, in part because of the bumpy, pothole-riddled streets and the generally unsavoury state into which downtown Detroit had fallen in the 1960s and '70s. The Detroit Renaissance Committee eventually yielded to economic realities and switched to an Indy car race for 1989.

Although the track was never a favourite of the Indy car drivers either, the event was a success. However, the pressures of real estate developments around the Renaissance Center forced

the organizers to move the race to Belle Isle on the Detroit River in 1992. The new semi-permanent circuit winds through the trees and pavilions of a city park and is generally well liked by drivers and teams, although the circuit presents few passing opportunities.

While its Indy car history dates back to just 1989, the Detroit Grand Prix has provided a number of memorable moments. Fittipaldi suffered

> **❝They threw the green [flag] and we went. What happened after that doesn't mean a thing.❞**
>
> *Team owner Roger Penske*

a flat tyre on the opening lap of the 1989 race, pitted and rejoined the race in last place. He then stormed the field to pass rookie driver Scott Pruett in the closing stages and win the race.

He won at Detroit the next year, but only after the race was stopped as Mario Andretti ploughed into an organizer's safety truck, and then Michael Andretti ploughed into his father. Neither were injured, but the race has to rank as the Andretti family's most embarrassing moment.

98

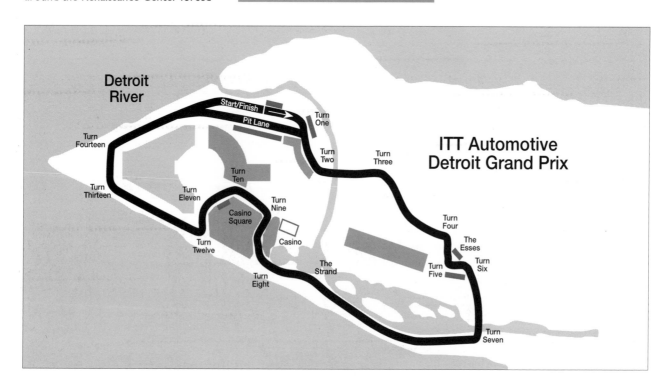

# RACE REPORT

After five weeks on the ovals, the Indy cars returned to a street course at the tricky Belle Isle circuit in Detroit. Although Mansell edged Fittipaldi and Tracy for the pole, it was clear the Penske-Chevies were going to be tough to beat, as evinced by Stefan Johansson's welcome return to the sharp end of the grid in fourth, while Bobby Rahal was fifth alongside sensational newcomer Andrea Montermini in the Euromotorsports '92 Lola-Chevy. Although Galles Racing's Al Unser Jr and Danny Sullivan were seventh and tenth on the grid, respectively, more would be heard from them on race day.

It was a strange race from the set-off. Mansell, beginning to get a little frustrated at his penchant for losing his hard-won pole advantage at the drop of the green flag, shook his fist in frustration as Fittipaldi burst past on the run to Turn One – with Tracy in tow. CART officials huddled and, 13 laps later, decided to give a stop 'n' go penalty to Fittipaldi for jumping the start. It was a penalty that caught everyone familiar with oval track starts by surprise, as the rule of thumb is the race starts when the green flag drops – no matter where the cars are relative to the start/finish line. Simple logic states that if the outside front row man jumps the start then it is up to the starter not to display the green flag.

"If there's something wrong with the start, they should throw the yellow," said an irate Roger Penske. "They threw the green and we went. What happened after that doesn't mean a thing."

The best (or worst) was yet to come. Fittipaldi crashed trying to regain ground; Tracy was penalized for speeding on pit road; Johansson and Mansell collided while disputing third place; and then Nigel crashed out of the race when he went off line avoiding a safety truck.

Thus Sullivan emerged in first place with Unser up his gearbox. The two lapped in tandem with Danny slowed by a leaky turbo, but Unser unable to force his way past on the twisty circuit. Nine laps from the finish, Al drew alongside his supposed team-mate as they raced down the Strand – a sweeping high speed section whose left side is marked by a series of rubber cones. Sullivan refused to yield and, in effect, forced Unser "out of bounds".

Having penalized drivers in practice and qualifying for hitting the cones, CART steward Wally Dallenbach felt duty bound to be consistent and assessed a stop 'n' go penalty to Unser. Robby Gordon emerged in second, albeit briefly as he had a flat tyre in the closing laps, enabling Raul Boesel to take yet another second place from Mario Andretti while the remarkable Montermini scooted around Rahal on the final lap to claim fourth. A furious Unser was followed by Galles team-mate Adrian Fernandez with Gordon, Tracy, Scott Goodyear, Mike Groff and Willy T Ribbs rounding out the top 12.

**99**

*Calm before the storm: Detroit's controversial start would have repercussions throughout the season.*

# PORTLAND INTERNATIONAL RACEWAY, PORTLAND, OREGON, JUNE 27th

## TRACK PROFILE

From its birth as the roadways and streets of a post-World War II housing estate, Portland International Raceway has grown to become a first-class racing circuit which annually hosts Oregon's largest sporting event: the Portland 200 Indy car race.

Since the first Indy car race at Portland in 1984, the facility has made rapid improvements with a new and expanded paddock, pit road and spectator bridge, while a number of hotels and restaurants have sprung up adjacent to the track. Add in the spectacular scenery, with Mt Hood rising to the east and now-flat-topped Mt St Helens to the north, and the delightful eateries which abound in and around Portland, and you have one of the most popular stops on the Indy car schedule.

The track itself is a challenging blend of high speed sections, including the 170 mph front straight and daunting Turn Seven/Eight chicane at the end of the curving back straight, the tight

### TRACK FACTS

- **Type of circuit:** road course
- **Length:** 1.95 miles
- **Laps:** 102
- **Distance driven:** 198.9 miles
- **No. of turns:** 9

"Festival" chicane on the front straightaway and the long, looping switchbacks that comprise the "infield" section of the circuit. Portland has also been the site of a couple of memorable Indy car races, including Al Unser Jr's first win in 1984, and Mario Andretti's win on Father's Day in 1985, when he passed his son Michael at the finish line to win by .07 seconds in what was the closest race in Indy car history (and remains so between father and son!).

## RACE REPORT

▶ In the final weekend of June the PPG Indy Car World Series made its first visit to a permanent road circuit in 1993 at Portland International Raceway. A flat but demanding track, Portland places an emphasis on straight-line speed with its two long straightaways, as well as high speed cornering with its series of sweeping turns at the west end of the circuit.

Having shown their stuff in qualifying at Detroit, the Penske cars quickly emerged as the machinery to beat at Portland, as Emerson Fittipaldi, Paul Tracy and Stefan Johansson dominated practice with hometown favourite Mark Smith not far behind in a '92 Penske. The only Lola to give the Penskes any serious competition belonged to Nigel Mansell and, when

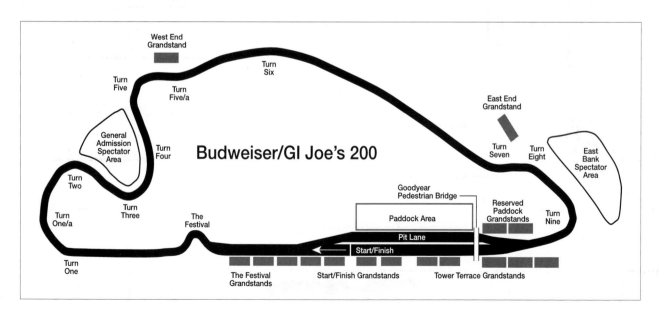

# "We fought hard, we were side by side, just inches apart."

*Mansell on being edged out by Fittipaldi in first place.*

Tracy blew an engine early in the final qualifying session, Nigel emerged on pole for the fourth time in 1993.

After the Detroit debacle, there was much nervous anticipation over the Portland start, but all came off smoothly and Mansell took his position at the head of a queue with Fittipaldi and, initially, Johansson leading Tracy from Mario Andretti and Smith. As the race settled in, Tracy took Johansson and Smith's fine run ended with a broken gearbox while Fittipaldi piled the pressure on Mansell. Driving hard as ever, Mansell kept Fittipaldi at bay.

"Nigel was defending his position as much as he could in a competitive, clean way," said Fittipaldi. "There were no tricks between us."

"We fought hard, we were side by side just inches apart," said Mansell. "The racing was hard, but very fair."

After 31 laps the pressure – and a slight brake imbalance – got to Mansell, who locked his brakes and slid into the cones marking the front straightaway chicane, handing the lead to Fittipaldi with Tracy up to second. Darkening skies had been approaching for some time and, just short of half distance the rains came, though more in the form of drizzle than a cloud burst.

Rain, shine or in-between, Fittipaldi motored along on his merry way to his second win of 1993, while Mansell eventually reclaimed second from Tracy after Johansson fell out with mechanical problems as Bobby Rahal edged Al Unser Jr and Mario Andretti for fourth. Slowed by an intermittent misfire, Raul Boesel could do no better than seventh but held off Robby Gordon and Mike Groff while Arie Luyendyk, Jimmy Vasser and Scott Goodyear completed the points-getters.

**The Penske samba**: *Emerson Fittipaldi's successes have created legions of Indy car racing fans in his native Brazil.*

## TRACK PROFILE

Held on the runways of Burke Lakefront Airport, against the backdrop of the city skyline, the Cleveland Grand Prix is the race that refuses to die. Owing to the rough and bumpy surface of the runways and taxiways, as well as the lengthy trek back and forth to the "paddock" (a parking lot fully ½ mile from the pits), the Cleveland race has never been a favourite among teams and drivers. But when the race was dropped from the tentative 1992 schedule, the local business community rallied around the race to boost the purse and improve the facility. The race's short-term future is now at least assured.

The circuit used to include a second chicane just past the pits, but in 1990 that transition from the runway to taxiway proved so severe that several cars crashed in the opening minutes of practice. The chicane was quickly eliminated so the track ran straight past the pits to the Turn One hairpin.

For all its shortcomings, Cleveland invariably puts on an entertaining race.

**TRACK FACTS**

| | |
|---|---|
| ● Type of circuit: | temporary road course |
| ● Length: | 2.369 miles |
| ● Laps: | 85 |
| ● Distance driven: | 201.37 miles |
| ● No. of turns: | 10 |

In large part this has to do with the wide racing surface afforded by the runways, which enables drivers to run two and three abreast through turns with little fear of hitting anything solid should they drop a wheel or two off course in the process. With long straightaways and wide, wide turns, the Cleveland circuit annually produces lap speeds topping 140 mph. The 1988 race was a classic as Mario Andretti, Danny Sullivan and Bobby Rahal traded the lead back and forth for 50 laps before Mario won one of his greatest victories.

## RACE REPORT

From the first permanent road course to the only temporary airport circuit on the schedule, the PPG Indy Car World Series moved east from Portland to Cleveland's Burke Lakefront Airport for the fastest non-oval track of the year.

Once again the Penske-Chevies quickly established themselves as favourites. Such was their superiority, that CART officials spent long hours pouring over the chassis in an effort to detect any "irregularities" such as a traction control system.

That was like searching for a needle in the proverbial haystack, and so Paul Tracy duly took his first pole of the season from Nigel Mansell, Emerson Fittipaldi and Stefan Johansson, with Scott Goodyear next up ahead of a resurgent Danny Sullivan, Al Unser Jr, Mark Smith, Teo Fabi and Bobby Rahal.

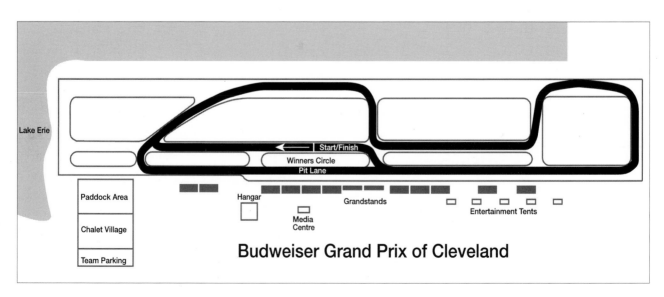

Lake Erie

Start/Finish

Winners Circle
Pit Lane

Paddock Area

Chalet Village

Team Parking

Hangar

Media Centre

Grandstands

Entertainment Tents

**Budweiser Grand Prix of Cleveland**

That may have been how it started, but it didn't last that way for long as Arie Luyendyk made an ill-fated effort to go around the outside of the pack in Turn One and punted Rahal from behind. Unphased, Rahal continued on his own circuitous route around the outside of the hairpin only to get clouted by Smith. The Miller Genuine Draft Lola then speared into the middle of the pack and all hell broke loose.

When it was over, Rahal and Roberto Guerrero were out, Luyendyk was in for a new nose and Unser, Goodyear and Boesel had dropped to the back of the field sporting various cosmetic damages.

Although Mansell had taken the lead from Tracy initially, the young Canadian soon stole back the spot and

## ❝This is the best race I've ever had.❞

*Paul Tracy, winner*

simply motored off to his second win of the year. End of story.

"Roger [Penske] let me know who was where and who I needed to be aware of," said Tracy. "Roger gave me everything I needed to know. This is the best race I've ever had. Thanks to a true team effort we dominated today."

Mansell, who'd sprained his wrist the previous day in a fall entering the press room, was left to fend off Fittipaldi. The two traded second places back and forth like a hot potato before the Brazilian finally wrenched the runner-up spot away from the Newman/Haas driver for good with

eight laps remaining to make it 1–2–4 for the Penske chassis as Johansson had his best result of the year.

A lap down along with Johansson were Mario Andretti, Robby Gordon, a still-misfiring Boesel and Teo Fabi. Brian Till brought still another Penske home in the top ten ahead of Luyendyk, Olivier Grouillard and Hiro Matsushita after Mark Smith's fine drive came to a spectacular end when his gearbox exploded in flames in front of the pits four laps shy of the chequered flag.

*Taking off: With the help of mentor Rick Mears, Paul Tracy led the Cleveland race and came of age.*

103

# TORONTO, ONTARIO, JULY 25th

## TRACK PROFILE

Since 1986, the Indy cars have been racing through the grounds of the Canadian National Exhibition Park on perhaps the best street circuit in the PPG Cup Series.

Somehow the track designers have managed to cram just about everything you could ask for in a circuit – a ³/₄ mile straightaway followed by a first-gear hairpin, several daunting high speed corners and a couple of medium speed bends – into this 1.78 mile, 11-turn circuit. That it's located a trolley ride away from one of North America's most cosmopolitan cities is the icing on the cake.

The Molson Indy Toronto, as it's known, has witnessed a number of dramatic races, none more so than the inaugural race where Bobby Rahal stormed back from a stop 'n' go penalty to a win that propelled him to the 1986

PPG Cup Series title. Similarly, Al Unser Jr took advantage of driving rain in 1990 to beat Michael Andretti and start a run of four wins that would lead to the national title.

Michael Andretti, however, made up for this by winning the '91 and '92 Toronto races and, with the '89 race already his, made it a hat-trick here.

| TRACK FACTS | |
|---|---|
| ● *Type of circuit:* | temporary road course |
| ● *Length:* | 1.78 miles |
| ● *Laps:* | 103 |
| ● *Distance driven:* | 183 miles |
| ● *No. of turns:* | 11 |

# RACE REPORT

The Penske stranglehold on the mid-season continued at Toronto when Paul Tracy scored a popular hometown victory from team-mate Emerson Fittipaldi, while Nigel Mansell failed to finish after perhaps his worst weekend since going Indy car racing.

Fittipaldi and Tracy traded fastest laps with Stefan Johansson throughout practice and qualifying before the Brazilian emerged on top in the final session. Tracy had to be content with the outside of the front row and the Swede slipped to sixth on the grid behind Bobby Rahal and Danny Sullivan. Mansell would start ninth after spearing into the Turn One wall on Friday in his

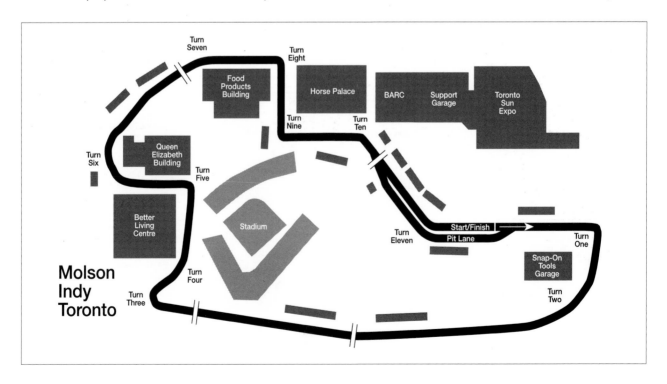

Molson Indy Toronto

back-up car, then wiping out his primary Lola on Saturday when he spun into the tyres lining Turn Six.

Fittipaldi got the jump on Tracy at the start, with Bobby Rahal heading Danny Sullivan, Johansson and an opportunistic Robby Gordon, who zipped from twelfth on the grid to sixth by virtue of a fearless move around a pack of cars in Turn One.

After a couple of full course yellows, Tracy got the drop on Fittipaldi to take the lead by out braking for the Turn Three hairpin, and began to pull free, while Emerson found himself fending off the advances of Sullivan, Rahal and Al Unser Jr. Back in the pack, Mansell battled briefly with Mario Andretti, Raul Boesel and Roberto Guerrero before retiring with a broken wastegate in his turbocharger.

"I had no power at all," said Mansell. "So I came into the pits to check what was going on and that's when I found out there was no way I could continue. But that's motor racing. It's the first time this year the car has

let me down, so I have no complaints."

Fittipaldi took the lead on the first round of pit stops when Tracy nearly stalled exiting the pit, but the Indy 500 winner later grazed the Turn Three wall while lapping an inattentive Hiro Matsushita and he was forced to make his second pit stop ahead of schedule. Tracy's second pit stop was flawless and he duly regained a lead he would never relinquish, while Fittipaldi slowed with gear selection problems. In fact, at the start of the final lap he shifted from third to fourth and the gear shift lever come off in his hand!

Fortunately for Fittipaldi, the third-placed Sullivan was too busy repulsing the advances of Rahal and Unser (who'd swapped positions on the final pit stop) to make a concerted bid for second and so Tracy and Emerson scored a second straight 1-2 for Penske. Fittipaldi's second place, coupled with Mansell's

dnf, boosted the two-time World Champion into the PPG points lead.

"What a great day for Canada, myself and my friends," said Tracy who, unbeknownst to many, had been under the weather most of the weekend. "It's a great feeling. This is the best race I've ever driven. I'm starting to smooth out and get some consistency. It was a lot of hard work. I had problems getting gears and Emerson was very tough. And I've had tonsillitis all week and my throat did get very dry during the race."

A regularly finisher now, Gordon outlasted Boesel for sixth while Andretti could do no better than eighth ahead of Goodyear, Guerrero and Jimmy Vasser as F-1 refuge Bertrand Gachot scored a single point in his Indy car debut with Dick Simon Racing.

**Hometown hero**: *Paul Tracy on the way to a popular win in the Toronto Molson Indy.*

# MICHIGAN INTERNATIONAL SPEEDWAY, BROOKLYN, MICHIGAN, AUGUST 1st

## TRACK PROFILE

Constructed during racing's boom years in the late 1960s, Michigan International Speedway was one of two virtually identical tracks built near Jackson, Michigan and College Station, Texas. In contrast to the symmetrical oval at Indianapolis, MIS is a D-shaped two-mile oval, with 18 degree banking in the turns, 12 degrees of banking on the curving front straightaway and five degrees on the 2242 foot long back straightaway.

Both Michigan and Texas World Speedway suffered financial setbacks in the early 1970s and Roger Penske stepped in to buy MIS. Penske has subsequently invested considerable sums of money into the circuit, and the facility is second to none in Indy car racing in amenities. Nevertheless, its location makes MIS susceptible to the brutal Michigan winters and the track remains notoriously rough, despite a repaving in 1986.

Like Phoenix and Milwaukee, Michigan hosted two Indy car races for a number of years: the Michigan 500 in early August and a 200 or 250 mile race in September. As with Phoenix and Milwaukee, however, scheduling pressures forced MIS to relinquish its September date in 1987.

Although Michigan International Speedway has been a fixture on the Indy car schedule for little more than 20 years, the Michigan 500 has developed its own unique atmosphere. For years, the race had an unmistakable aura of danger looming over it, for the combination of high speeds and the bumpy track produced some of the most spectacular accidents in Indy car racing history.

The inaugural Michigan 500 in 1981 was halted for an hour when an accident on pit road resulted in a tremendous fire; the 1984 race included half a dozen potentially lethal accidents involving the likes of Bobby Rahal, Al Unser Jr, Pancho Carter and Chip Ganassi yet, remarkably, only Ganassi was seriously injured and he

| TRACK FACTS | |
|---|---|
| ● *Type of circuit:* | **superspeedway** |
| ● *Length:* | **2 miles** |
| ● *Laps:* | **250** |
| ● *Distance driven:* | **500 miles** |
| ● *No. of turns:* | **4: banked at 18°** |

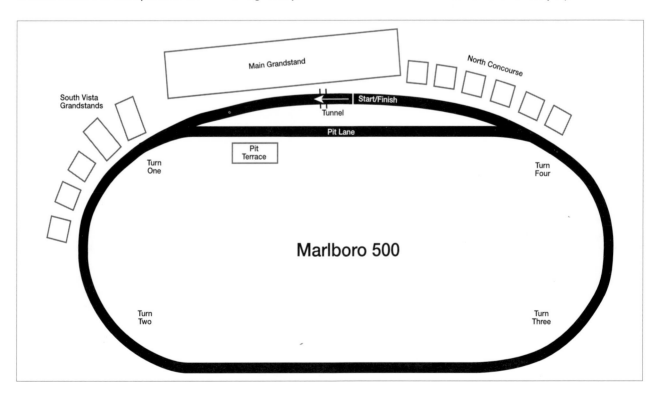

eventually recovered. The danger was somewhat alleviated by the extensive repaving in 1986, and the Michigan 500 has come to signal the start of the annual "silly season", when rumours of drivers, teams and sponsors making big changes for the coming season reaches a fever pitch.

MIS also has a way of producing dramatic winners. In 1983, John Paul Jr out-duelled Rick Mears to win his first – and only – Indy car victory, before he was subsequently convicted of conspiracy charges in connection with his father's drug dealing operations. The 1985 Michigan 500 saw Emerson Fittipaldi score his first Indy car victory and Johnny Rutherford scored his 27th – and perhaps final – Indy car win in the Michigan 500 the following year.

# RACE REPORT

▶ Having already won a mile oval race in his rookie season, Nigel Mansell put another large feather in his cap with a commanding win on the fearsome high banks at Michigan International Speedway, leading virtually from start to finish to reclaim the top spot emphatically in the PPG points race. Underlining the domination of Newman/Haas Racing was the fact that Mario Andretti finished second, the only man on the same lap as Mansell at the finish.

From the start, it was clear the KMart/Havoline Lolas would be the ones to beat around MIS' bumpy banks. In the first practice session Mansell and Andretti topped 232 mph while nobody else got above 229 mph – all weekend. That was the good news. The bad news was that Mansell was decidedly unhappy about the condition of the race track, the racing surface of which takes a fearsome beating from November to March in the frigid Michigan winters.

## "The track beats you down. When someone gets killed it's too late."

*Mansell's pre-race assessment of the bumpy circuit*

"I'm certainly not happy and I don't mind voicing my opinion," said Nigel. "The track beats you down. When someone gets killed it's too late."

Qualifying saw Mansell turn a 233.462 mph only to have Mario reply with a new world's closed course record of 234.275 mph. Next best were Arie Luyendyk and Raul Boesel at 229 mph. The heretofore dominant Penskes struggled with Paul Tracy a reasonable fifth fastest but Fittipaldi a lowly 15th on the grid after switching to his spare car when the primary one proved unmanageable.

Having used the latest development Ford/Cosworth XBs to demolish the opposition in qualifying, Newman/Haas switched back to standard engines for the race and, if anything, were more dominant than ever. Although Mario led the first 27 laps, Mansell took over on the 28th tour and only lost the lead once – to Luyendyk during a pit stop sequence – for the remainder of the

day. So dominant was Mansell that he even put his team-mate a lap down at one stage. And while Mario eventually got the lap back, the outcome was never in doubt.

Luyendyk came home a somewhat fortunate third, having struggled to keep up with Boesel for most of the race. But in the late going Boesel stopped for fuel only to have the track go yellow a few laps later, enabling Arie to gain the advantage. Goodyear too had rotten luck with yellows and lost a couple of laps on pit stops, while Teo Fabi was the first Chevy-powered driver home after Tracy blew up. Guerrero, Al Unser Jr, Bobby Rahal, Willy T Ribbs, Scott Brayton and David Kudrave completed the points getters ahead of a disappointed Fittipaldi, who completed one of his most dismal showings in years in thirteenth place, thirteen laps off the pace.

*Speedway ace: Arie Luyendyk led the chase of the Newman/Haas Lola/Fords at Michigan.*

107

# NEW HAMPSHIRE INTERNATIONAL SPEEDWAY, LOUDON, NEW HAMPSHIRE, AUGUST 8th

## TRACK PROFILE

The newest mile oval on the PPG Cup Series schedule, New Hampshire International Speedway held its first Indy car race in 1992 to rave reviews. Set in the foothills of New Hampshire's White Mountains a two-hour drive from Boston, NHIS is a state-of-the art oval that was built by the Bahre family without a firm commitment from the organizers or NASCAR that they would schedule a major race there.

NASCAR ran its Busch series there in 1990 and '91, CART added NHIS to its schedule in 1992, then NASCAR scheduled an NHIS Winston Cup event in 1993.

New Hampshire is something of a mixture of Milwaukee and Nazareth. Like Milwaukee, it's a symmetrical track featuring long straights and tight corners. Although the corners are tighter than Milwaukee's, they are more steeply banked. This produces good racing in that cars have to brake for the corners – creating passing opportunities

| TRACK FACTS | |
|---|---|
| ● Type of circuit: | superspeedway |
| ● Length: | 1.058 miles |
| ● Laps: | 200 |
| ● Distance driven: | 211.6 miles |
| ● No. of turns: | 4: banked at 12° |

– while the banking enables competitors to run side-by-side.

Like Nazareth, NHIS also features elevation changes. The exit of Turn Two is slightly uphill, while the entrance to Turn Three is slightly downhill. This raises the back straightaway about 12 feet above the level of the front straight, and provides better viewing for the fans in the 65,000 seat grandstand.

Bobby Rahal was the inaugural winner in 1992, setting the track record of 133.621 – an average speed which even Mansell couldn't better in '93.

## RACE REPORT

▶ Nigel Mansell celebrated his 40th birthday in memorable fashion, surpassing Paul Tracy and Emerson Fittipaldi in an enthralling race around the mile oval at New Hampshire International Speedway that was Indy car racing at its absolute best.

For most of the weekend, however, it looked as if Raul Boesel was finally going to get his just desserts. He dominated practice just as he had at the last mile oval at Milwaukee. Come qualifying, though, and the "other" Brazilian lost the fine edge on his Duracell Lola/Ford and had to settle for the outside of the front row. Mansell came through to his first pole on a one mile oval; Goodyear and Tracy shared second row – as they had at Milwaukee.

Although Mansell got the jump at

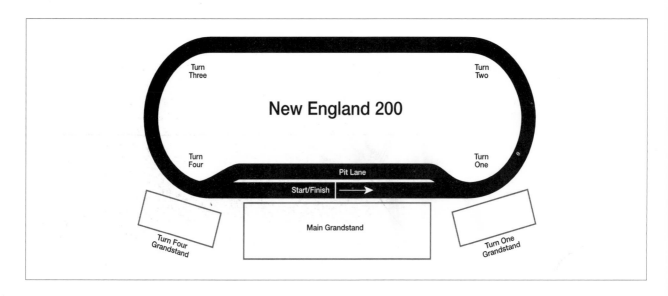

New England 200

Turn Three

Turn Two

Turn Four

Turn One

Pit Lane

Start/Finish

Turn Four Grandstand

Main Grandstand

Turn One Grandstand

the start, it wasn't long before he was under pressure from Tracy as Boesel faded slightly. Goodyear made an initially strong showing as well before fading, while Fittipaldi – who'd been plagued by turbo-boost problems in qualifying – methodically worked his way to the front.

Roberto Guerrero was another player as well, running just out of touch with Mansell, Tracy and Boesel until he was mistakenly called in too early during a caution period and the Budweiser Lola-Chevy lost most of a lap in the process. In fact, Roberto found himself running flat out to keep from being lapped by Mansell. And as Nigel looked for a way around his former Formula 3 rival, Tracy and Fittipaldi closed on Red Five, with Emerson shoving Paul back to third in the process.

At the start of Lap 95 Mansell finally got the better of Roberto. Heading into Turn Three half a lap later Nigel tucked in behind Marco Greco's oft-lapped car. Fittipaldi followed suit only to have Guerrero sail back around the lot of them with Tracy in tow, taking the lead in the process!

And Paul looked like keeping the top spot as well, for Mansell later dropped to third behind Fittipaldi when

## "If you've got to turn 40, this is the way to do it!… It's the most thoroughbred racing I've ever done in my life."

*Mansell, winner*

a wheel nut jammed on his second pit stop. However, Mansell eventually tigered his way around Emerson and set sail for Tracy, Boesel by now having spun into the wall in Turn Two and Mario Andretti and Goodyear having also exited the race after coming together in Turn Four.

Although Nigel could close on Tracy, the Canadian's oval track experience showed as he spurted free of the World Champion each time they encountered a group of slower cars. Come Lap 190 however, and Mansell successfully trapped Tracy behind a slower car in Turn Two and took the lead – only to find himself stuck behind yet another car entering Turn Three and have Tracy whisk back into the lead as if nothing had happened!

But Nigel is nothing if not a fast learner, and he returned the favour when the two lapped Stefan Johansson entering Turn One with just five laps remaining. While Tracy gained the advantage initially, Mansell exited the

corner with greater momentum and seized the lead heading into Turn Three. Amazingly, he faced a virtually clear track for the final few tours and duly came home a delighted victor.

"If you've got to turn 40 this is the way to do it!" beamed Mansell. "I've got no problems here today admitting that I learned some moves I didn't know about…This is pure racing. You can race in a different way on ovals which you can't do on road courses. You can take different lines, go side-by-side. It's the most thoroughbred racing I've ever done in my life."

Guerrero scored an encouraging fourth for the Budweiser/King team ahead of Gordon and Brayton. Brian Till, Mike Groff and Olivier Grouillard (bouncing back from a crash on Saturday to earn a PPG point for Euromotorsport Racing) completed the points.

*Jinxed?:* Rahal (who finished 7th in a Lola after his Rahal/Hogan chassis dnq at the Indy 500) about to be lapped by Gordon (who finshed 5th), with Jimmy Vasser (9th) and Jeff Wood (dnf) to the rear.

# ROAD AMERICA, ELKHART LAKE, WISCONSIN, AUGUST 22nd

## TRACK PROFILE

This four-mile road course in the heart of Wisconsin's Kettle Moraine country is a sentimental favourite of every American sports car racer.
Constructed in the mid-1950s, Road America has hosted every major American road racing series – from the old United States Road Racing Championship to the Can-Am, Formula 5000 and Trans-Am series.

Although the track features three 180-mph straightaways, the pace at Road America is somehow more gentle – a reflection perhaps of the days when sports car racing was a gentleman's sport. In those days everyone retired at the end of the day to talk racing at nearby Seibken's Hotel and Resort, or stayed at the track to sample Road America's famous food, ranging from fresh cooked corn-on-the-cob to bratwurst sandwiches.

The Indy cars have been racing at Road America since 1982 and from the very first race, a pattern was set. Fuel economy is often a deciding factor at Road America, given the high fuel consumption that comes from accelerating to 180 mph three times a lap and the fact that the pits are located at the top of a hill; a car that runs out of fuel has no chance of coasting back to the pits.

Thus Mexican driver Hector Rebaque won his only Indy car race at Road America in 1982 when Al Unser ran out of fuel on the final lap. Danny Sullivan roared back from a 20-second deficit to catch and pass a sputtering Michael Andretti on the final lap in 1989, and Andretti won the 1991 race on the basis of flawless pit-work and fuel consumption strategy.

## TRACK FACTS

- **Type of circuit:** road course
- **Length:** 4 miles
- **Laps:** 50
- **Distance driven:** 200 miles
- **No. of turns:** 11

# RACE REPORT

▶ Nigel Mansell's two-race winning streak came to a screeching halt at bucolic Road America, where the Penske PC-22/Chevy reasserted its dominant road racing form with Paul Tracy scoring his third victory of the season from pole.

But Road America was no walkover for the Marlboro Penske team. On Friday morning Tracy emerged battered and bruised from a 180-mph crash caused by a rear suspension failure, while team-mate Emerson Fittipaldi struggled with turbo boost problems, just as he had in New Hampshire. Their problems enabled Newman/Haas Racing to take control of proceedings, with Mansell claiming the provisional pole and Mario Andretti a strong third ahead of Raul Boesel. Tracy was an impressive

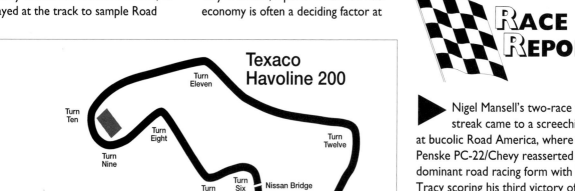

Texaco Havoline 200

second fastest, despite putting in a minimum of laps in his spare car in order to rest his sprained ankle.

Sure enough, when it came to the crunch on Saturday, Tracy gained pole from Mansell and Andretti while Boesel edged Fittipaldi for the fourth spot. But at four miles long – and with the pits situated at the top of a hill – Road America places as much emphasis on fuel management as speed. So while it was certain that Tracy had the speed to win, the big question on race day was whether he had a similar advantage in fuel economy.

From the first laps it was apparent that only a miscalculation on fuel – or a mechanical failure – stood between Tracy and the win. Pulling away from Mansell, Andretti and Boesel at up to a second a lap, Tracy quickly established a five-second cushion. When a quick first pit stop staked him to a further ten seconds, the race for first place was all but finished. Rather than easing up to conserve fuel, Tracy stretched his margin to as much as 18 seconds before the second pit stop, and eventually came home nearly half a minute ahead of Mansell – this despite

## "It's just a question of picking up real valuable points today."

*Second-placed Mansell, lagging far behind winner, Tracy*

being in considerable discomfort in the latter stages of the race.

"My [right] foot began to feel numb and I had to be very careful every time I touched the brake pedal because of the numbness," Paul explained. "So I used the engine and the gearbox to slow down a lot more than usual; that put an extra strain on them but they held up."

Although Mansell held sway in second place, Mario Andretti gradually chipped away at his lead until the second Kmart/Havoline Lola slowed with a broken valve spring.

"As soon as I knew of Mario's problem I sort of backed off a bit," said Mansell. "The gap had opened up anyway over half-distance and I couldn't maintain that even when I was pushing real hard. It's just a question of picking up real valuable points today."

Andretti's demise enabled Bobby Rahal to come through to third, the reigning PPG having emerged the leader of an entertaining scrap involving Robby

Gordon, Arie Luyendyk and Fittipaldi, who continued to be slowed by boost problems. Boesel made an early pit stop during a full course yellow in an effort to steal a march on the field in fuel economy, but then had to work his way back up from 18th spot. He was able to get back to fourth place eventually while Fittipaldi moved up to fifth after Gordon retired with overheating problems and Luyendyk suffered a punctured tyre in the closing laps.

Eddie Cheever, making a return to Indy car racing with Dick Simon Racing, was thus promoted to sixth place ahead of Scott Brayton and Teo Fabi. Luyendyk was eventually awarded ninth place ahead of Scott Goodyear, Christian Danner (making just his second start of the season in the Euromotorsports Lola/Chevy) and Willy T Ribbs.

*Not out of the woods yet:* Teo Fabi and Hall/VDS Racing went winless in 1993.

111

# PACIFIC PLACE, VANCOUVER, BRITISH COLUMBIA, AUGUST 29th

## TRACK PROFILE

The city of Vancouver, set on a narrow isthmus between the Pacific Ocean and the Coast Mountains, is surely among the most dramatic locations imaginable for an Indy car race. The race track itself, alas, is not one of the better ones on the schedule.

It features a series of tight chicanes and one hair-raising 180 mph blast through a sweeping turn past the pits, and then along a rough and bumpy stretch leading to a first-gear hairpin.

The inaugural race in 1990 was a tragic one as a safety worker, who had fallen while pushing a stalled car out of harm's way in the blind Turn Four chicane, was run over and killed by a car driven by Willy T Ribbs. By contrast, the 1992 race was an almost comic affair, that featured crashes galore but, fortunately, no serious injuries among a veritable Who's Who of Indy car racing including Bobby Rahal, Stefan Johansson, Al Unser Jr and Emerson Fittipaldi.

| TRACK FACTS | |
|---|---|
| ● *Type of circuit:* | temporary road course |
| ● *Length:* | 1.677 miles |
| ● *Laps:* | 100 |
| ● *Distance driven:* | 167.7 miles |
| ● *No. of turns:* | 10 |

## RACE REPORT

▶ Indy car racing's most successful street racer, Al Unser Jr, scored a classic victory on Vancouver's tricky street circuit, timing his second pit stop to perfection and then outlasting Bobby Rahal on the final run to the chequered flag. The win was Unser's 19th in Indy car competition and his first since the 1992 Indianapolis 500. It was also Al's 15th Indy car victory on a temporary road course.

The race strengthened Nigel Mansell's seeming stranglehold on the

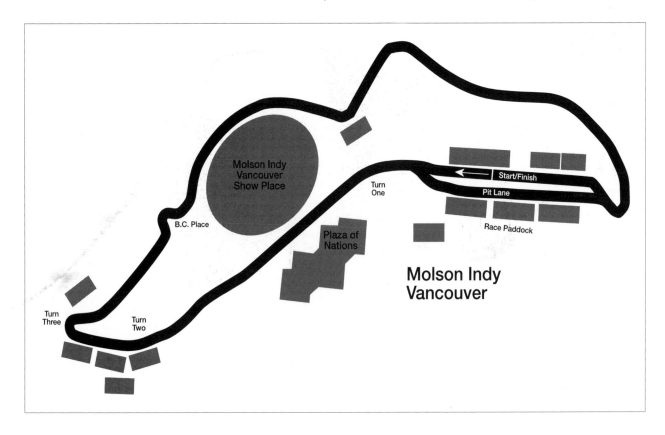

Molson Indy Vancouver Show Place

B.C. Place

Turn One

Start/Finish

Pit Lane

Race Paddock

Plaza of Nations

Turn Three

Turn Two

Molson Indy Vancouver

PPG points lead, as the World Champion finished in sixth place, one spot ahead of Emerson Fittipaldi, his closest rival in the title chase. Paul Tracy, who has earned more points than anyone since midseason, suffered electrical problems in the early stages of the race and failed to score at all.

Although the Penske PC22-Chevrolets of Tracy, Fittipaldi and Johansson were 1-2-3 on Friday's provisional grid, Scott Goodyear took his second pole of the season from Rahal in the waning moments of qualifying on Saturday. Both drivers were benefiting from revised aerodynamics on their '93 Lolas, including a new undertray and radiator deflectors, while Goodyear also had the latest Ford/Cosworth XB. Mansell recovered from a lacklustre day on Friday to take third on the grid ahead of Tracy, who had trouble getting a clear lap in qualifying.

Next up was Unser's Valvoline Lola-Chevy alongside Robby Gordon, while little Andrea Montermini and the Euromotorsports team continued to humble many of the big names with a fine run to seventh on the grid. Bothered by handling problems, Fittipaldi and Johansson wound up tenth and eleventh, respectively.

A series of minor shunts on the first lap eliminated a number of backmarkers, but Montermini's day was also ruined when he bent his right front wing in a minor contact with Unser, while Gordon dropped out with a broken halfshaft. Thereafter, the race bore a striking resemblance to the final laps of the New Hampshire event as Goodyear, Tracy and Rahal swapped places, with Unser looking on in fourth.

"That was a lot of fun fighting with Scott and Paul," said Rahal. "I locked my brakes into Turn Ten, then a few laps later he did the same thing and I got by down the straight."

When the going finally settled down, it was Rahal who took command of the race from Unser, while Goodyear dropped back to a distant third and Tracy fell far behind after a

stop to repair the wiring to his alternator. Mansell dropped to tenth after stalling his car on the first pit stop, while Johansson's crew did sterling work and got the Swede up to fourth place on the same stop.

Although Unser was glued to Rahal's gearbox, he couldn't muster the speed to pass the Miller Genuine Draft car, so opted to sit back and put the race in the hands of the Galles Racing pit crew. Rahal made his final stop on Lap 65. Unser stayed out for two more laps, taking advantage of a light fuel load, hot tyres and a lack of traffic to build a useful cushion of time. Thus while his pit stop was marginally quicker than Rahal's, he emerged with a five-second lead on the defending PPG champion and ran off to a perfectly judged victory.

"I saw Bobby's pit board come out and I thought, 'I hope my guys didn't show him mine,'" said Unser. "They did a good job of that and I was able to pull out a nice cushion on empty tanks. Then my guys won the race with a great pit stop; they made the pass."

Goodyear was all set for his first trip to the podium in 1993 when he lost the use of third and fifth gears and watched helplessly as Johansson swept past with one lap remaining. Mario Andretti came home fifth ahead of Mansell, who benefited from an excellent second pit stop to leap-frog past Fittipaldi, Teo Fabi and Raul Boesel and claim sixth place, while Danny Sullivan came home tenth ahead of Roberto Guerrero and Hiro Matsushita.

*Indy cars take the A-train each year at Vancouver.*

# MID-OHIO SPORTS CAR COURSE, LEXINGTON, OHIO, SEPTEMBER 12th

## TRACK PROFILE

Now America's most modern racing facility, Mid-Ohio was an overgrown club track for much of its life before Jim Trueman purchased the property in 1980. Trueman immediately went to work turning the basic circuit into a showcase, upgrading the pits, garage area and spectator amenities. Following Trueman's untimely death in 1986, his wife, Barbara, continued his legacy, putting the final touches to the track with major repaving, widening and an upgraded safety programme in 1990.

Mid-Ohio is also one of America's most fabled road racing facilities and, like Road America, has been the sight of virtually every major road racing series

### TRACK FACTS

| | |
| --- | --- |
| ● **Type of circuit:** | **road course** |
| ● **Length:** | **2.25 miles** |
| ● **Laps:** | **89** |
| ● **Distance driven:** | **199.3 miles** |
| ● **No. of turns:** | **13** |

**The Esses**

Nissan Pedestrian Bridge

Budweiser Pedestrian Bridge

**Grandstands**

Observation Mound

Observation Mound

Goodyear Bridge

Start/Finish

Pit Lane

Turn One

Garages

Pond

The Carousel

## Pioneer Electronics 200

Keyhole

Observation Mound

in its time. Its serpentine layout, sudden and severe elevation changes, and compact layout make it a favourite for spectators, thousands of whom jam the S-bends at the end of the long straightaway each year – mainly to cheer local favourite Bobby Rahal.

# RACE REPORT

▶ Nigel Mansell came to the Pioneer 200 at Mid-Ohio looking to clinch his first PPG championship and left with Emerson Fittipaldi breathing down his neck. Paul Tracy and Raul Boesel were eliminated from title contention by the events of the day, which saw the Canadian crash while leading and Boesel finish fourth, inches behind Scott Goodyear and Robby Gordon.

The weekend had begun in fine style for Mansell, who earned his sixth pole to tie Teo Fabi's record for the most poles by a rookie driver in a season. But Nigel had to fight for this one, just edging Tracy and Fittipaldi after the three swapped fastest laps during the final ten minutes of qualifying. First Fittipaldi set a fastest time of 1:08.579. Tracy replied with a 1:08.564 moments later only to run out of fuel while trying to go even faster. That left the final drama to Mansell, who roared around in 1:08.428 to gain the pole.

The start at Mid-Ohio is always entertaining. Owing to a shortish pit straightaway, the race is started in the middle of the back stretch, which funnels the field into a roller coaster series of S-bends. Traditionally, if the driver on the outside of the front row gets a good start, he is able to stay on the outside of the pole sitter through the first right hander, thus gaining the upper hand on the ensuing left hander.

At best it's the stuff of very close racing, but when Mansell and Tracy ran through the turns side-by-side it was "too-close" racing. Mansell's left front wheel banged off Tracy's right rear and the Newman/Haas Lola's suspension buckled. Nigel slowed and was engulfed by the field, including Arie Luyendyk, who clipped the Kmart/Havoline car's right front wing, sending it fluttering into the air.

"It was very unprofessional," said Mansell. "He [Tracy] chopped right across me and took me out."

"I've always been able to take the outside line going into the S's," said Tracy. "I got by ahead of Nigel and I guess his left front tyre tagged my rear."

By the time Mansell's crew effected repairs, he was two laps behind and out of the running. Meanwhile, Tracy was demolishing the field à la Phoenix and Road America. Alas, as at Phoenix, he stumbled over lapped traffic – in the form of Scott Pruett – and crashed out of the race on Lap 22.

That left Fittipaldi with a narrow lead on Scott Goodyear and Al Unser Jr. Goodyear tried to forge past the Marlboro car on the restart following Tracy's crash, but fell to third for his troubles. Unser took up the challenge only to run foul of Fittipaldi in the S-bends and slide into the back of

**“It was very unprofessional. He chopped right across me and took me out.”**

*Mansell 12th on Tracy, dnf*

Goodyear's car, trashing the Valvoline Lola's nose wing.

When the fibreglass settled, Fittipaldi held a commanding lead over Goodyear, Robby Gordon, Raul Boesel and Luyendyk, who had charged through the field after replacing the tyre cut in his encounter with Mansell.

In shades of Vancouver, Goodyear slowed perceptibly after his last pit stop as his final set of tyres created a handling imbalance, and Gordon swept past. Boesel moved in for the kill, but could not find a way past the Mackenzie car and the race ended with Goodyear, Boesel and a closing Luyendyk nose-to-tail behind Fittipaldi and Gordon. Bobby Rahal was a quiet sixth ahead of Mario Andretti, while Unser recovered from

his off-road excursion to finish seventh ahead of Scott Brayton.

Jimmy Vasser, who ran as high as fifth at one point, had to make an extra pit stop after running low on fuel and finished tenth ahead of a down-on-power Willy T Ribbs while Mansell's recovery drive carried him to twelfth for the final point of the day.

*Would-be champions beware: 1992 and 1993 saw PPG points leaders Bobby Rahal and Nigel Mansell suffer setbacks at Mid-Ohio. While Mansell manfully pulled backed through the field for a single point, Rahal crashed out of the race altogether on the 4th lap in '92, giving Michael Andretti one last chance to overhaul him in the overall PPG points.*

# NAZARETH SPEEDWAY, PENNSYLVANIA, SEPTEMBER 19th

## TRACK PROFILE

Like a number of other tracks, Nazareth started out as a dirt track, albeit one in a special location – the hometown of the Andretti family. In 1986, however, Roger Penske purchased the facility and began a major upgrade designed to make it suitable to Indy car and other major professional racing series.

The track is the most idiosyncratic on the PPG Cup Series. Not quite a mile in length, Nazareth features three distinctly different turns, ranging from the flat-out kink of Turn One, to the wide-open Turn Two that falls downhill on the exit, and Turn Three which features a downhill entry and a steep, uphill exit. In all, there is a 34-foot elevation change on the track, with the back straightaway accounting for most of the downhill change, and the hill from Turn Three to Turn One the uphill portion.

Racing at Nazareth is fast, furious and not a little dangerous as the elevation changes and blind corners keep drivers on their toes every inch of the way. One Nazareth safety feature that has been copied elsewhere, including Indianapolis, is a dedicated warm-up lane – for cars just exiting the pits in practice and during the race – separated from the racing surface by a strip of grass.

## TRACK FACTS

| | |
|---|---|
| ● Type of circuit: | tri oval |
| ● Length: | 1 mile |
| ● Laps: | 200 |
| ● Distance driven: | 200 miles |
| ● No. of turns: | 3 |

116

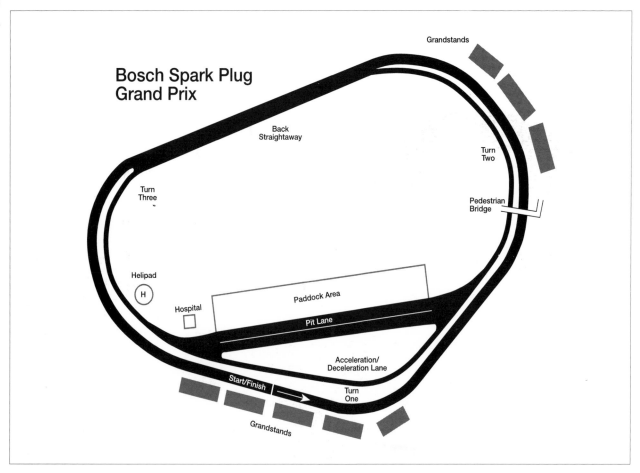

Bosch Spark Plug Grand Prix

Given its position on the schedule in October, Nazareth is often a pivotal event in the PPG Cup Series. Emerson Fittipaldi clinched the 1989 title with a win at Nazareth; the following season Al Unser Jr also clinched his PPG Cup Series title at Nazareth albeit in decidedly different fashion. Late in the race he was unwittingly involved in an accident between Arie Luyendyk and Danny Sullivan that sent him hard into the Turn Three wall. He learned he was the 1990 PPG Cup Series champion in a hospital in nearby Easton, Pennsylvania!

# RACE REPORT

▶ Mansell clinched the 1993 PPG Indy Car World Series title at Nazareth Speedway in convincing fashion, leading the final 154 laps of the Bosch Spark Plug Grand Prix. Nigel's lead over Fittipaldi in the PPG points swelled to an insurmountable 25 points. With the World Championship still technically undecided, Mansell thus became the first driver in history to be champion of Formula One and Indy cars simultaneously.

At Nazareth Mansell faced another hurdle in his metamorphosis from F1 to Indy car driver: a one-day weekend. The decision had been made earlier in the year to limit the Nazareth schedule to Saturday and Sunday in the interest of reduced costs. When rain forced the cancellation of Saturday's practice and qualifying, officials decided to form the starting grid on the basis of PPG points – with Mansell on pole, Fittipaldi second, Paul Tracy third, Raul Boesel fourth etc, and give each driver two half-hour practice sessions on Sunday morning.
The practice was not without drama, as Mansell's primary car developed a water leak and he was forced into his backup. But quick work by the

**❝I want to congratulate Nigel. He did a fantastic job this year and he surprised everybody on the ovals.❞**

*Emerson Fittipaldi showing the sporting nature of Indy car drivers...*

Newman/Haas crew got the primary Lola-Ford/Cosworth ready in time for the race. After one false start, the field was given the green flag the second time around and Fittipaldi and Tracy roared by Mansell into the lead. When Boesel slashed past on the approach to Turn Three, Mansell found himself down to fourth place in the space of less than a mile.
Although Tracy eventually closed on and passed Fittipaldi, it was Mansell who really came alive once the race settled down. He re-passed Boesel on Lap 27, moved around Fittipaldi on Lap 45 and then took Tracy for the lead on Lap 47.
"I had a slight problem with the car – a slight understeer – and I couldn't keep up with the pace," said Mansell. "Then Raul came past and I was down to fourth and I thought 'Well, that's not too clever.' I was able to rethink and redrive the car as it was, and then my car started to come into a little better balance. And then we had a great race in progress."
Tracy made an early pit stop in an effort to cure his suddenly oversteering car, while Fittipaldi stuck it out until Lap 70, hoping for a caution period that never came, and fell to fourth. On the move were Scott Goodyear and Arie Luyendyk, who moved from ninth and

eighth on the grid to second and third, respectively, by the first pit stop.
Such was Mansell's pace that Scott and Arie were the only unlapped drivers by mid-distance. However, Luyendyk's car began oversteering at this stage and he slowly dropped back through the field as Tracy and Robby Gordon surged into contention. In the end, however, they were no match for Mansell who lapped everyone but Goodyear on the way to his fourth consecutive oval track win, and his fifth win of the season.
"It makes you feel so proud," said Mansell of his thoughts on winning the championship. "The feelings I have are exactly the same, if not better, than the feelings I had when I won the World Championship last year. And I think last year I had a lot of things going my way. Number one, I didn't have a major accident at the second race. And I didn't have to undergo an operation during the course of last year. And there's no question we had some great backing and machinery behind us. What makes it so special is how close it was, and I can't thank Carl [Haas] and Paul [Newman] enough for making a very, very special dream come true."

*"I was disappointed that my car just went loose," said Fittipaldi who travelled home fifth, allowing Mansell to clinch the PPG title.*

117

**ROUND 16**     **FULL RACE RESULTS – PAGES 120-123**

# LAGUNA SECA RACEWAY, MONTEREY, CALIFORNIA, OCTOBER 3rd

## TRACK PROFILE

Another of America's historic road courses, Laguna Seca is located on the US Army's Fort Ord, just a few miles from scenic Monterey and Carmel, California. From its birth in the 1950s, Laguna Seca was famous for its high speeds and spectacular elevation changes, most notably the "Corkscrew"

that drops precipitously through a left/right turn sequence.

By the late 1980s Indy cars were lapping the 1.9-mile track in well under a minute, so a major reconstruction project was undertaken that eliminated the daunting high-speed section running from Turns One to Three in favour of a slower, but equally challenging infield

loop that added $\frac{3}{10}$ of a mile and 20 seconds to each lap.

After Teo Fabi won the inaugural Indy car race at Laguna Seca in 1983, Bobby Rahal won four straight Indy car races from 1984 to 87 while Danny Sullivan won both the first race on the revised layout and an emotional 1990 race, his final drive for Penske Racing.

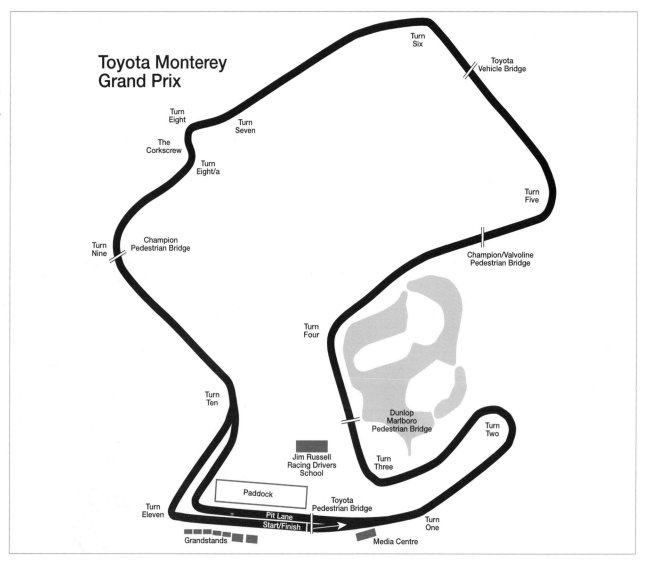

Toyota Monterey Grand Prix

## TRACK FACTS

| | |
|---|---|
| ● Type of circuit: | road course |
| ● Length: | 2.214 miles |
| ● Laps: | 84 |
| ● Distance driven: | 185.98 miles |
| ● No. of turns: | 11 |

# RACE REPORT

► Paul Tracy put the cap to his first full season of Indy car racing with a dominant win, beating Penske Racing team-mate Emerson Fittipaldi and Arie Luyendyk to score his fifth win of the year and match Nigel Mansell in the win column for 1993. Mansell's euphoric celebration of his PPG Cup was tempered slightly at Laguna Seca when he dropped out of fourth place after colliding with Mark Smith while trying to lap the Arciero car in the latter stages of the race.

A heavy fog shrouded the race track on Sunday morning, but the atmosphere eventually cleared enough to start the race some forty-five

**❝…it was physically difficult just to even keep my body from being thrown out of the car.❞**

*Tracy on winning the race without a seat belt*

minutes behind schedule. Tracy wasted no time in blasting into the lead from Fittipaldi, and the two Penskes pulled free of Mansell, Sullivan and Luyendyk as Johansson struggled to come to grips with a loose piece of carbon-fibre that had become entangled in his pedals.

Luyendyk eventually worked his way around Sullivan and Mansell, lost ground on his first pit stop and proceded to repass the pair of them. But the moment he got by Sullivan the Molson Lola-Chevy slowed with a broken exhaust header and, when Mansell ran into the back of rookie Scott Sharp's Penske exiting Turn Eleven, Luyendyk had all the room he needed to consolidate third place.

Up front, however, things were a little more hectic. While battling through lapped traffic, Tracy inadvertently opened the clasp securing his seat belts. Tossed around like a rag doll in the Penske thereafter, he was hard pressed to keep Fittipaldi behind him. "I'd never tried to drive without belts before," said Tracy. "With all the elevation changes and high speed turns it was physically difficult just to keep my body from being thrown out of the car."

Tracy had just about resigned himself to making a pit stop to refasten his belts when Fittipaldi had to take evasive action while lapping Hiro Matsushita, and spun into the infield in a billowing cloud of dust. "I spun and went cross country in the desert," said Fittipaldi. Miraculously, he kept his engine going and rejoined, but he'd lost all hope of catching his team-mate. Fittipaldi thus came home a distant second but well clear of Luyendyk, with Scott Goodyear charging through from ninth on the grid to claim fourth place ahead of Al Unser Jr.

Troubled all day by the foreign object bouncing around in the pedals, Johansson took sixth place ahead of a down-on-power Bobby Rahal, while Teo Fabi eventually got the best of Mario Andretti after a duel for eighth place. Robby Gordon was an unusually quiet tenth ahead of Raul Boesel, who ran out of fuel on the last lap, while Fernandez finished twelfth.

*Mansell's day and season ended rather unceremoniously when he tangled with Smith in Turn Two 13 laps from the finish. The force of the contact spun the steering wheel from Mansell's grip, reinjuring the wrist he had sprained at Cleveland and he was forced to retire.*

119

# 1993 PPG INDYCAR WORLD SERIES RACE RESULTS & DRIVER PERFORMANCE CHART

Nigel Mansell was never lower than second place in the PPG Cup standings this season. He led after Round 1, in Australia. After Round 2, at Phoenix (Mansell dns because of his accident during practice ) he trailed Mario Andretti 32-21 points. Mansell regained the lead in Round 3 at Long Beach. After Round 9, at Toronto (Mansell dnf), he trailed Fittipaldi 105-102 points. Mansell regained the lead yet again in Round 10 at Michigan and never lost it after that race.

## Indy car points system

| FINAL POS | POINTS | |
|---|---|---|
| 1 | 20 | |
| 2 | 16 | |
| 3 | 14 | CART awards points far deeper into the field than with F-1, down to twelfth place in fact, on a 20-16-14-12-10-8-6-5-4-3-2-1 basis. In addition, the pole winner is also awarded a single point, as is the driver who leads the most laps in a race. Thus a "clean sweep" of pole, most laps led, and race win nets a driver 22 PPG points. |
| 4 | 12 | |
| 5 | 10 | |
| 6 | 8 | |
| 7 | 6 | |
| 8 | 5 | |
| 9 | 4 | |
| 10 | 3 | |
| 11 | 2 | |
| 12 | 1 | |
| POLE POSITION | 1 | |
| MOST LAPS LEAD | 1 | |

## PPG Indycar World Series Round 1
### Australian FAI IndyCar Grand Prix - *Surfers Paradise*

| FINAL POS | GRID POS | DRIVER | LAPS | POINTS | TOTAL POINTS |
|---|---|---|---|---|---|
| 1 | 1 | Nigel Mansell | 65 | 21 | 21 |
| 2 | 2 | Emerson Fittipaldi | 65 | 17 | 17 |
| 3 | 4 | Robby Gordon | 65 | 14 | 14 |
| 4 | 6 | Mario Andretti | 65 | 12 | 12 |
| 5 | 5 | Arie Luyendyk | 65 | 10 | 10 |
| 6 | 13 | Bobby Rahal | 64 | 8 | 8 |
| 7 | 16 | Eddie Cheever | 64 | 6 | 6 |
| 8 | 8 | Raul Boesel | 64 | 5 | 5 |
| 9 | 12 | Teo Fabi | 64 | 4 | 4 |
| 10 | 7 | Scott Goodyear | 63 | 3 | 3 |
| 11 | 24 | Hiro Matsushita | 63 | 2 | 2 |
| 12 | 18 | Stefan Johansson | 63 | 1 | 1 |

Winning time: 1hr 52m 2.886s.
Winning average speed: 97.284mph.
Margin of victory: 5.113s. 5 lead changes, 2 drivers.

## PPG Indycar World Series Round 2
### Valvoline 200 - *Phoenix*

| FINAL POS | GRID POS | DRIVER | LAPS | POINTS | TOTAL POINTS |
|---|---|---|---|---|---|
| 1 | 2 | Mario Andretti | 200 | 20 | 32 |
| 2 | 6 | Raul Boesel | 199 | 16 | 21 |
| 3 | 9 | Jimmy Vasser | 197 | 14 | 14 |
| 4 | 13 | Al Unser Jr | 197 | 12 | 12 |
| 5 | 8 | Teo Fabi | 196 | 10 | 14 |
| 6 | 10 | Arie Luyendyk | 195 | 8 | 18 |
| 7 | 15 | Scott Pruett | 194 | 6 | 6 |
| 8 | 22 | David Kudrave | 193 | 5 | 5 |
| 9 | 11 | Mark Smith | 192 | 4 | 4 |
| 10 | 17 | Hiro Matsushita | 187 | 3 | 5 |
| 11 | 24 | Marco Greco | 183 | 2 | 2 |
| 12 | 25 | Ross Bentley | 183 | 1 | 1 |

Winning time: 1hr 36m 53.630s.
Winning average speed: 123.847mph.
Margin of victory: 22.378s. 3 lead changes, 3 drivers.

## PPG IndyCar World Series Round 3
### Toyota Grand Prix - *Long Beach*

| FINAL POS | GRID POS | DRIVER | LAPS | POINTS | TOTAL POINTS |
|---|---|---|---|---|---|
| 1 | 2 | Paul Tracy | 105 | 21 | 22 |
| 2 | 11 | Bobby Rahal | 105 | 16 | 24 |
| 3 | 1 | Nigel Mansell | 105 | 15 | 36 |
| 4 | 7 | Teo Fabi | 105 | 12 | 26 |
| 5 | 18 | Roberto Guerrero | 104 | 10 | 10 |
| 6 | 23 | Robbie Buhl | 104 | 8 | 8 |
| 7 | 15 | Scott Pruett | 103 | 6 | 12 |
| 8 | 12 | Danny Sullivan | 103 | 5 | 5 |
| 9 | 10 | Eddie Cheever | 103 | 4 | 10 |
| 10 | 14 | Mark Smith | 103 | 3 | 7 |
| 11 | 19 | Arie Luyendyk | 103 | 2 | 20 |
| 12 | 9 | Raul Boesel | 102 | 1 | 22 |

Winning time: 1hr 47m 36.418s.
Winning average speed: 93.089mph.
Margin of victory: 12.658s. 5 lead changes, 2 drivers.

## PPG IndyCar World Series Round 4
### 77th Indianapolis 500 - *Indianapolis*

| FINAL POS | GRID POS | DRIVER | LAPS | POINTS | TOTAL POINTS |
|---|---|---|---|---|---|
| 1 | 9 | Emerson Fittipaldi | 200 | 20 | 37 |
| 2 | 1 | Arie Luyendyk | 200 | 17 | 37 |
| 3 | 8 | Nigel Mansell | 200 | 14 | 50 |
| 4 | 3 | Raul Boesel | 200 | 12 | 34 |
| 5 | 2 | Mario Andretti | 200 | 11 | 43 |
| 6 | 11 | Scott Brayton | 200 | 8 | 8 |
| 7 | 4 | Scott Goodyear | 200 | 6 | 10 |
| 8 | 5 | Al Unser Jr | 200 | 5 | 17 |
| 9 | 17 | Teo Fabi | 200 | 4 | 30 |
| 10 | 24 | John Andretti | 200 | 3 | 3 |
| 11 | 6 | Stefan Johansson | 199 | 2 | 2 |
| 12 | 23 | Al Unser | 199 | 1 | 1 |

Winning time: 3hr 10m 49.860s.
Winning average speed: 157.207mph.
Margin of victory: 2.862s. 24 lead changes, 12 drivers.

## PPG IndyCar World Series Round 5
### Miller Genuine Draft 200 - *Milwaukee*

| Final Pos | Grid Pos | Driver | Laps | Points | Total Points |
|---|---|---|---|---|---|
| 1 | 7 | Nigel Mansell | 200 | 20 | 70 |
| 2 | 1 | Raul Boesel | 200 | 18 | 52 |
| 3 | 2 | Emerson Fittipaldi | 200 | 14 | 51 |
| 4 | 9 | Bobby Rahal | 200 | 12 | 36 |
| 5 | 18 | Al Unser Jr | 198 | 10 | 27 |
| 6 | 6 | Scott Brayton | 198 | 8 | 16 |
| 7 | 10 | Roberto Guerrero | 198 | 6 | 16 |
| 8 | 13 | Jimmy Vasser | 196 | 5 | 19 |
| 9 | 14 | Teo Fabi | 195 | 4 | 34 |
| 10 | 8 | Robby Gordon | 193 | 3 | 17 |
| 11 | 21 | Willy T Ribbs | 193 | 2 | 2 |
| 12 | 15 | Olivier Grouillard | 191 | 1 | 1 |

Winning time: 1hr 48m 8.245s.
Winning average speed: 110.970mph.
Margin of victory: 0.514s. 9 lead changes, 6 drivers.

## PPG IndyCar World Series Round 6
### ITT Automotive Detroit Grand Prix - *Belle Isle Park*

| Final Pos | Grid Pos | Driver | Laps | Points | Total Points |
|---|---|---|---|---|---|
| 1 | 10 | Danny Sullivan | 77 | 21 | 26 |
| 2 | 11 | Raul Boesel | 77 | 16 | 68 |
| 3 | 9 | Mario Andretti | 77 | 14 | 57 |
| 4 | 6 | Andrea Montermini | 77 | 12 | 12 |
| 5 | 5 | Bobby Rahal | 77 | 10 | 46 |
| 6 | 7 | Al Unser Jr | 77 | 8 | 35 |
| 7 | 21 | Adrian Fernandez | 77 | 6 | 6 |
| 8 | 8 | Robby Gordon | 77 | 5 | 22 |
| 9 | 3 | Paul Tracy | 76 | 4 | 26 |
| 10 | 22 | Scott Goodyear | 76 | 3 | 13 |
| 11 | 24 | Mike Groff | 75 | 2 | 2 |
| 12 | 25 | Willy T Ribbs | 75 | 1 | 3 |

Winning time: 1hr 56m 43.678s.
Winning average speed: 83.116mph.
Margin of victory: 12.206s. 4 lead changes, 4 drivers.

## PPG IndyCar World Series Round 7
### Budweiser/G.I. Joe's 200 - *Portland, Oregon*

| Final Pos | Grid Pos | Driver | Laps | Points | Total Points |
|---|---|---|---|---|---|
| 1 | 2 | Emerson Fittipaldi | 102 | 21 | 72 |
| 2 | 1 | Nigel Mansell | 102 | 17 | 88 |
| 3 | 4 | Paul Tracy | 102 | 14 | 40 |
| 4 | 15 | Bobby Rahal | 101 | 12 | 58 |
| 5 | 9 | Al Unser Jr | 101 | 10 | 45 |
| 6 | 5 | Mario Andretti | 101 | 8 | 65 |
| 7 | 11 | Raul Boesel | 100 | 6 | 74 |
| 8 | 10 | Robby Gordon | 100 | 5 | 27 |
| 9 | 12 | Mike Groff | 100 | 4 | 6 |
| 10 | 14 | Arie Luyendyk | 99 | 3 | 40 |
| 11 | 22 | Jimmy Vasser | 99 | 2 | 21 |
| 12 | 16 | Scott Goodyear | 98 | 1 | 14 |

Winning time: 2hr 03m 54.620s.
Winning average speed: 96.312mph.
Margin of victory: 4.359s. 6 lead changes, 3 drivers.

## PPG IndyCar World Series Round 8
### Budweiser Grand Prix - *Cleveland*

| Final Pos | Grid Pos | Driver | Laps | Points | Total Points |
|---|---|---|---|---|---|
| 1 | 1 | Paul Tracy | 85 | 22 | 62 |
| 2 | 3 | Emerson Fittipaldi | 85 | 16 | 88 |
| 3 | 2 | Nigel Mansell | 85 | 14 | 102 |
| 4 | 4 | Stefan Johansson | 84 | 12 | 15 |
| 5 | 11 | Mario Andretti | 84 | 10 | 75 |
| 6 | 20 | Robby Gordon | 84 | 8 | 35 |
| 7 | 12 | Raul Boesel | 84 | 6 | 80 |
| 8 | 9 | Teo Fabi | 84 | 5 | 39 |
| 9 | 13 | Brian Till | 83 | 4 | 4 |
| 10 | 15 | Arie Luyendyk | 83 | 3 | 43 |
| 11 | 17 | Olivier Grouillard | 82 | 2 | 3 |
| 12 | 21 | Hiro Matsushita | 81 | 1 | 6 |

Winning time: 1hr 34m 27.254s.
Winning average speed: 127.913mph.
Margin of victory: 18.090s. 5 lead changes, 2 drivers.

121

## PPG IndyCar World Series Round 9
### Molson Indy - *Toronto*

| Final Pos | Grid Pos | Driver | Laps | Points | Total Points |
|---|---|---|---|---|---|
| 1 | 2 | Paul Tracy | 103 | 21 | 83 |
| 2 | 1 | Emerson Fittipaldi | 103 | 17 | 105 |
| 3 | 4 | Danny Sullivan | 103 | 14 | 40 |
| 4 | 3 | Bobby Rahal | 103 | 12 | 70 |
| 5 | 7 | Al Unser Jr | 103 | 10 | 55 |
| 6 | 12 | Robby Gordon | 103 | 8 | 43 |
| 7 | 6 | Raul Boesel | 103 | 6 | 86 |
| 8 | 13 | Mario Andretti | 102 | 5 | 80 |
| 9 | 10 | Scott Goodyear | 102 | 4 | 18 |
| 10 | 14 | Roberto Guerrero | 102 | 3 | 19 |
| 11 | 17 | Jimmy Vasser | 101 | 2 | 23 |
| 12 | 15 | Bertrand Gachot | 101 | 1 | 1 |

Winning time: 1hr 53m 58.951s
Winning average speed: 95.510mph.
Margin of victory: 13.023s. 3 lead changes, 2 drivers.

## PPG IndyCar World Series Round 10
### Marlboro 500 - *Michigan*

| Final Pos | Grid Pos | Driver | Laps | Points | Total Points |
|---|---|---|---|---|---|
| 1 | 2 | Nigel Mansell | 250 | 21 | 123 |
| 2 | 1 | Mario Andretti | 250 | 17 | 97 |
| 3 | 3 | Arie Luyendyk | 249 | 14 | 57 |
| 4 | 4 | Raul Boesel | 248 | 12 | 98 |
| 5 | 6 | Scott Goodyear | 247 | 10 | 28 |
| 6 | 8 | Teo Fabi | 246 | 8 | 47 |
| 7 | 11 | Roberto Guerrero | 245 | 6 | 25 |
| 8 | 17 | Al Unser Jr | 245 | 5 | 60 |
| 9 | 16 | Bobby Rahal | 243 | 4 | 74 |
| 10 | 13 | Willy T Ribbs | 243 | 3 | 6 |
| 11 | 7 | Scott Brayton | 241 | 2 | 18 |
| 12 | 19 | David Kudrave | 239 | 1 | 6 |

Winning time: 2hr 39m 24.131s
Winning average speed: 188.203mph.
Margin of victory: 9.434s. 3 lead changes, 3 drivers.

## PPG IndyCar World Series Round 11
### New England 200 - *New Hampshire*

| Final Pos | Grid Pos | Driver | Laps | Points | Total Points |
|---|---|---|---|---|---|
| 1 | 1 | Nigel Mansell | 200 | 21 | 144 |
| 2 | 4 | Paul Tracy | 200 | 17 | 100 |
| 3 | 13 | Emerson Fittipaldi | 200 | 14 | 119 |
| 4 | 5 | Roberto Guerrero | 199 | 12 | 37 |
| 5 | 14 | Bobby Gordon | 199 | 10 | 53 |
| 6 | 7 | Scott Brayton | 198 | 8 | 26 |
| 7 | 9 | Bobby Rahal | 197 | 6 | 80 |
| 8 | 15 | Al Unser Jr | 197 | 5 | 65 |
| 9 | 11 | Jimmy Vasser | 194 | 4 | 27 |
| 10 | 21 | Brian Till | 194 | 3 | 7 |
| 11 | 16 | Mike Groff | 194 | 2 | 8 |
| 12 | 19 | Olivier Grouillard | 192 | 1 | 4 |

Winning time: 1hr 37m 33.033s.
Winning average speed: 130.148mph.
Margin of victory: 0.453s. 4 lead changes, 2 drivers.

## PPG IndyCar World Series Round 12
### Texaco Halvoline 200 - *Road America*

| Final Pos | Grid Pos | Driver | Laps | Points | Total Points |
|---|---|---|---|---|---|
| 1 | 1 | Paul Tracy | 50 | 22 | 122 |
| 2 | 2 | Nigel Mansell | 50 | 16 | 160 |
| 3 | 10 | Bobby Rahal | 50 | 14 | 94 |
| 4 | 4 | Raul Boesel | 50 | 12 | 110 |
| 5 | 5 | Emerson Fittipaldi | 50 | 10 | 129 |
| 6 | 15 | Eddie Cheever | 50 | 8 | 18 |
| 7 | 13 | Scott Brayton | 49 | 6 | 32 |
| 8 | 16 | Teo Fabi | 49 | 5 | 52 |
| 9 | 11 | Arie Luyendyk | 49 | 4 | 61 |
| 10 | 7 | Scott Goodyear | 49 | 3 | 31 |
| 11 | 14 | Christian Danner | 49 | 2 | 2 |
| 12 | 22 | Willy T Ribbs | 48 | 1 | 7 |

Winning time: 1hr 41m 20.689s.
Winning average speed: 118.408mph.
Margin of victory: 27.459s. No lead changes

## PPG IndyCar World Series Round 13
### Molson Indy - *Vancouver*

| Final Pos | Grid Pos | Driver | Laps | Points | Total Points |
|---|---|---|---|---|---|
| 1 | 5 | Al Unser Jr | 102 | 20 | 85 |
| 2 | 2 | Bobby Rahal | 102 | 17 | 111 |
| 3 | 11 | Stefan Johansson | 102 | 14 | 19 |
| 4 | 1 | Scott Goodyear | 102 | 13 | 44 |
| 5 | 14 | Mario Andretti | 102 | 10 | 107 |
| 6 | 3 | Nigel Mansell | 101 | 8 | 168 |
| 7 | 10 | Emerson Fittipaldi | 101 | 6 | 135 |
| 8 | 9 | Teo Fabi | 101 | 5 | 57 |
| 9 | 8 | Raul Boesel | 101 | 4 | 114 |
| 10 | 15 | Danny Sullivan | 100 | 3 | 43 |
| 11 | 13 | Roberto Guerrero | 100 | 2 | 39 |
| 12 | 22 | Hiro Matsushita | 96 | 1 | 7 |

Winning time: 1hr 49m 52.652s.
Winning average speed: 91.794mph.
Margin of victory: 11.199s. 3 lead changes, 4 drivers.

## PPG IndyCar World Series Round 14
### Pioneer Electronics 200 - *Mid-Ohio*

| Final Pos | Grid Pos | Driver | Laps | Points | Total Points |
|---|---|---|---|---|---|
| 1 | 3 | Emerson Fittipaldi | 89 | 21 | 156 |
| 2 | 15 | Robby Gordon | 89 | 16 | 69 |
| 3 | 5 | Scott Goodyear | 89 | 14 | 58 |
| 4 | 4 | Raul Boesel | 89 | 12 | 126 |
| 5 | 8 | Arie Luyendyk | 89 | 10 | 71 |
| 6 | 14 | Bobby Rahau | 89 | 8 | 119 |
| 7 | 10 | Mario Andretti | 89 | 6 | 113 |
| 8 | 6 | Al Unser Jr | 89 | 5 | 90 |
| 9 | 18 | Scott Brayton | 88 | 4 | 36 |
| 10 | 9 | Jimmy Vasser | 88 | 3 | 30 |
| 11 | 22 | Willy T Ribbs | 88 | 2 | 9 |
| 12 | 1 | Nigel Mansell | 87 | 2 | 170 |

Winning time: 1hr 56m 59.188s.
Winning average speed: 102.217mph.
Margin of victory: 16.668s. 1 lead change, 2 drivers.

## PPG IndyCar World Series Round 15
### Bosch Spark Plug Grand Prix - *Nazareth*

| Final Pos | Grid Pos | Driver | Laps | Points | Total Points |
|---|---|---|---|---|---|
| 1 | 1 | Nigel Mansell | 200 | 21 | 191 |
| 2 | 10 | Scott Goodyear | 200 | 16 | 74 |
| 3 | 4 | Paul Tracy | 198 | 14 | 136 |
| 4 | 9 | Robby Gordon | 198 | 12 | 81 |
| 5 | 2 | Emerson Fittipaldi | 198 | 10 | 166 |
| 6 | 5 | Bobby Rahal | 196 | 8 | 127 |
| 7 | 14 | Stefan Johansson | 196 | 6 | 35 |
| 8 | 8 | Arie Luyendyk | 195 | 5 | 76 |
| 9 | 3 | Raul Boesel | 194 | 4 | 130 |
| 10 | 15 | Eddie Cheever | 192 | 3 | 21 |
| 11 | 11 | Teo Fabi | 191 | 2 | 59 |
| 12 | 19 | Mark Smith | 189 | 1 | 8 |

Winning time: 1hr 15m 37.273s
Winning average speed: 158.686mph
Margin of victory: 19.042s. 3 lead changes, 3 drivers

## PPG IndyCar World Series Round 16
### Toyota Monterey Grand Prix - *Laguna Seca*

| Final Pos | Grid Pos | Driver | Laps | Points | Total Points |
|---|---|---|---|---|---|
| 1 | 2 | Paul Tracy | 84 | 21 | 157 |
| 2 | 1 | Emerson Fittipaldi | 84 | 17 | 183 |
| 3 | 5 | Arie Luyendyk | 84 | 14 | 90 |
| 4 | 9 | Scott Goodyear | 84 | 12 | 86 |
| 5 | 12 | Al Unser Jr | 84 | 10 | 100 |
| 6 | 7 | Stefan Johansson | 83 | 8 | 43 |
| 7 | 10 | Bobby Rahal | 83 | 6 | 133 |
| 8 | 11 | Teo Fabi | 83 | 5 | 64 |
| 9 | 6 | Mario Andretti | 83 | 4 | 117 |
| 10 | 14 | Robby Gordon | 83 | 3 | 84 |
| 11 | 13 | Raul Boesel | 82 | 2 | 132 |
| 12 | 24 | Adrian Fernandez | 82 | 1 | 7 |

Winning Time: 1hr 44m 58.169s
Winning average speed: 106.303mph
Margin of victory: 27.491s. 3 lead changes, 2 drivers

# 1993 PPG IndyCar World Series Driver Performance Chart

| Rank | Driver | Points | Starts | Fin. | Top Fin. | Times LED | Laps LED | Laps [2112 total] | Miles [3658.902] |
|---|---|---|---|---|---|---|---|---|---|
| 1 | Nigel Mansell | 191 | 15 | 12 | 1 | 22 | 603 | 1839 | 3319.632 |
| 2 | Emerson Fittipaldi | 183 | 16 | 14 | 1 | 14 | 270 | 2024 | 3511.484 |
| 3 | Paul Tracy | 157 | 16 | 9 | 1 | 21 | 756 | 1657 | 2754.145 |
| 4 | Bobby Rahal | 133 | 15 | 13 | 2 | 2 | 58 | 1673 | 2792.404 |
| 5 | Raul Boesel | 132 | 16 | 13 | 2 | 4 | 103 | 2013 | 3543.352 |
| 6 | Mario Andretti | 117 | 16 | 13 | 1 | 10 | 139 | 1995 | 3518.445 |
| 7 | Al Unser Jr | 100 | 16 | 12 | 1 | 2 | 55 | 1877 | 3278.285 |
| 8 | Arie Luyendyk | 90 | 16 | 11 | 2 | 4 | 15 | 1681 | 3075.022 |
| 9 | Scott Goodyear | 86 | 16 | 10 | 2 | 5 | 53 | 1832 | 3331.380 |
| 10 | Robby Gordon | 84 | 15 | 9 | 2 | 3 | 7 | 1764 | 3085.111 |
| 11 | Teo Fabi | 64 | 16 | 13 | 4 | 0 | 0 | 1909 | 3265.666 |
| 12 | Danny Sullivan | 43 | 15 | 9 | 1 | 1 | 30 | 1216 | 1973.524 |
| 13 | Stefan Johansson | 43 | 15 | 7 | 3 | 0 | 0 | 1219 | 2208.079 |
| 14 | Roberto Guerrero | 39 | 13 | 6 | 4 | 0 | 0 | 1382 | 2283.167 |
| 15 | Scott Brayton | 36 | 16 | 11 | 6 | 0 | 0 | 1643 | 2969.495 |
| 16 | Jimmy Vasser | 30 | 12 | 8 | 3 | 0 | 0 | 1305 | 2131.238 |
| 17 | Eddie Cheever | 21 | 9 | 6 | 6 | 0 | 0 | 777 | 1553.898 |
| 18 | Andrea Montermini | 12 | 4 | 1 | 4 | 0 | 0 | 128 | 257.391 |
| 19 | Scott Pruett | 12 | 6 | 3 | 7 | 0 | 0 | 482 | 756.640 |
| 20 | Willy T Ribbs | 9 | 13 | 10 | 10 | 0 | 0 | 1485 | 2608.714 |
| 21 | Robbie Buhl | 8 | 10 | 5 | 6 | 0 | 0 | 871 | 1369.510 |
| 22 | Mark Smith | 8 | 12 | 5 | 9 | 0 | 0 | 872 | 1470.273 |
| 23 | Mike Groff | 8 | 6 | 2 | 9 | 1 | 1 | 599 | 956.302 |
| 24 | Adrian Fernandez | 7 | 5 | 2 | 7 | 0 | 0 | 322 | 527.638 |
| 25 | Brian Till | 7 | 8 | 5 | 9 | 0 | 0 | 778 | 1286.951 |
| 26 | Hiro Matsushita | 7 | 16 | 15 | 10 | 0 | 0 | 1979 | 3444.550 |
| 27 | David Kudrave | 6 | 7 | 3 | 8 | 0 | 0 | 859 | 1191.504 |
| 28 | Olivier Grouillard | 4 | 11 | 8 | 11 | 0 | 0 | 1169 | 1937.962 |
| 29 | John Andretti | 3 | 1 | 1 | 10 | 1 | 2 | 200 | 500.000 |
| 30 | Marco Greco | 2 | 13 | 5 | 11 | 0 | 0 | 1083 | 1681.850 |
| 31 | Christian Danner | 2 | 3 | 1 | 11 | 0 | 0 | 138 | 398.471 |
| 32 | Ross Bentley | 1 | 11 | 9 | 12 | 0 | 0 | 1219 | 1994.059 |
| 33 | Al Unser | 1 | 1 | 1 | 12 | 2 | 15 | 199 | 497.500 |
| 34 | Bertrand Gachot | 1 | 1 | 1 | 12 | 0 | 0 | 101 | 179.780 |
| 35 | Kevin Cogan | 0 | 4 | 3 | 13 | 1 | 4 | 398 | 902.279 |
| 36 | Lyn St James | 0 | 6 | 3 | 13 | 0 | 0 | 632 | 1145.932 |
| 37 | Mauricio Gugelmin | 0 | 3 | 1 | 13 | 0 | 0 | 289 | 465.098 |
| 38 | Buddy Lazier | 0 | 10 | 4 | 14 | 0 | 0 | 786 | 1318.234 |
| 39 | Dominic Dobson | 0 | 3 | 2 | 14 | 0 | 0 | 358 | 799.700 |
| 40 | Gary Brabham | 0 | 1 | 1 | 14 | 0 | 0 | 62 | 173.290 |
| 41 | Jeff Wood | 0 | 8 | 2 | 15 | 0 | 0 | 373 | 682.796 |
| 42 | Didier Theys | 0 | 2 | 2 | 15 | 0 | 0 | 274 | 661.834 |
| 43 | Davy Jones | 0 | 1 | 1 | 15 | 0 | 0 | 197 | 492.500 |
| 44 | Jonny Unser | 0 | 4 | 2 | 17 | 0 | 0 | 367 | 548.216 |
| 45 | Gary Bettenhausen | 0 | 1 | 1 | 17 | 0 | 0 | 197 | 492.500 |
| 46 | Stephan Gregoire | 0 | 1 | 1 | 19 | 1 | 1 | 195 | 487.500 |
| 47 | Tony Bettenhausen | 0 | 1 | 1 | 20 | 0 | 0 | 195 | 487.500 |

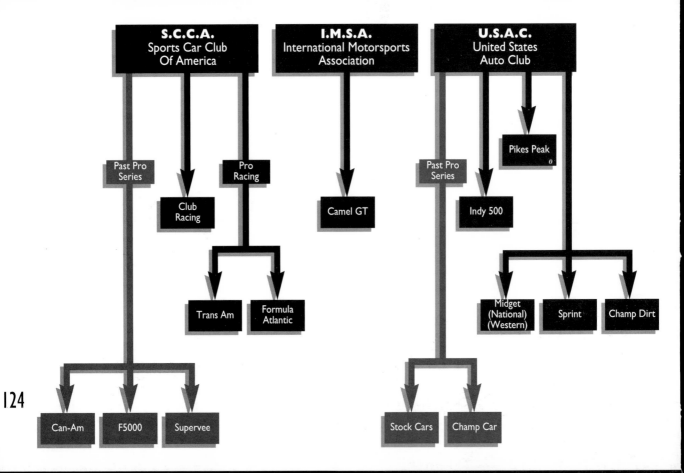

**S.C.C.A.**
Sports Car Club Of America

**I.M.S.A.**
International Motorsports Association

**U.S.A.C.**
United States Auto Club

Past Pro Series

Pro Racing

Club Racing

Camel GT

Pikes Peak

Past Pro Series

Indy 500

Trans Am

Formula Atlantic

Midget (National) (Western)

Sprint

Champ Dirt

124

Can-Am

F5000

Supervee

Stock Cars

Champ Car

# Indy car: glossary

**AAA**: The American Automobile Association sanctioned the national championship from the early 1900s to 1955. Today the AAA focuses on the concerns of the average motorist and has no direct involvement in motorsports.

**ACCUS**: The Automobile Competition Committee for the United States is the official arm of the FIA in the US. ACCUS is made up of representatives from the major American racing organizations – CART, NASCAR, NHRA, USAC, SCCA together with selected "at large" members.

**BALANCE**: Describes the handling characteristics of a race car; when the car neither understeers nor oversteers it is said to be "well balanced" or "neutral".

**BOOST**: The amount of pressure created by the turbocharger as it forces compressed air into the engine's intake manifold. Measured in inches of mercury, the higher the boost, the greater the engine's power output.

**BULLRING**: A comparatively short oval track. In Indy car racing, the term is used to differentiate mile ovals such as Phoenix and Milwaukee from the longer Indianapolis and Michigan superspeedways. Outside of Indy car racing, however, the term refers to the numerous ¼, ⅜ and ½ mile ovals that form the backbone of American racing.

**CAN-AM**: The Can-Am (short for Canadian-American Challenge Cup Series) debuted in 1966 as a series for unlimited sports cars and rapidly rose to prominence on the international scene with series sponsorship from Johnson's Wax. McLaren Racing utterly dominated the Can-Am from 1967 to 1971; even Jackie Stewart and a factory Lola were unable to break their stranglehold on the series title. Porsche entered the fray with its monstrous 917/10 and 917/30 turbos and demolished all opposition in 1972 and '73, sending the cost of competition out of sight in the bargain. The series enjoyed a brief resurgence in the early '80s with turbocharging banned and engines limited to five litres. By 1985 it had

become little more than a series for wealthy amateurs and was subsequently abandoned by the SCCA, although the Can-Am name lives on in a minor league, one-make sports car series.

**CART**: Championship Auto Racing Teams was formed in 1978 by Roger Penske and Pat Patrick who, like a number of Indy car team owners, were dissatisfied with USAC's administration of the sport. From 1979 to 1990 CART operated outside of the bounds of the international motorsport community but in 1990 joined ACCUS.

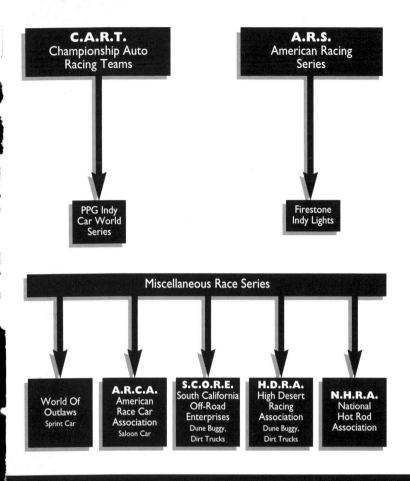

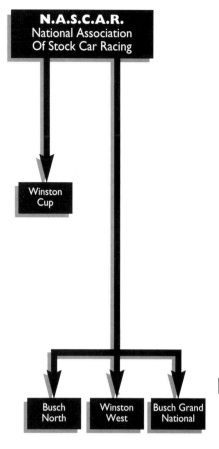

125

**DNF/DNS/DNQ**: Did not finish; did not start; did not qualify. (Shorthand also used in several sections of this book.)

**DIRTY AIR**: Refers to the turbulence created by a car passing through the air at high speed and which can have a dramatic impact (usually negative) on the aerodynamic effectiveness of the following car.

**DOWNFORCE**: Aerodynamic pressure created by wings, sidepods and undertrays that pushes down on the car and thus enables it to go through turns at a higher rate of speed than would otherwise be possible.

**DRAFT**: Following another car closely at high speed on a straightaway. With the lead car effectively punching a hole in the air, the second car faces less wind resistance. Thus the second car can run at the same speed as the lead car using less throttle, then pass the lead car by accelerating and pulling out of the draft. Also known as slipstreaming and "getting a tow."

**FIRESTONE INDY LIGHTS**: Official training ground of PPG Series, FIL was founded by Pat Patrick in 1986 as a bridge between the junior formulae of the time and Indy cars. FIL is a "spec series", in that only one kind of engine (4·2 litre Buick V-6) and chassis (Lola 93B) are permitted, in order to reduce costs and equalize competition. Past champions include Paul Tracy and Robby Buhl.

**FISA**: Federation Internationale de Sport Automotive is the Paris-based organization which governs the world of motorsports.

**FLAT BOTTOM**: When the underside of a racing car is flat and, therefore, does not use ground effects to create downforce. Flat bottom chassis are usually mandated in the rules to slow cornering speeds. F1 cars are now flat bottom; the Firestone Indy Lights cars are also required to use flat bottom design; Indy cars are not.

**FORMULA 5000**: Class of open wheeled racing cars powered by five-litre stock block engines that was very popular in Europe,

North America, Australia and New Zealand in the 1970s. With Mario Andretti, Al Unser, Alan Jones, Brian Redman, Jody Scheckter, Jackie Oliver, David Hobbs and Graham McRae all competing at various times, F-5000 was arguably the premier professional open wheel series in North America at times. The formula passed from the scene in 1977, however, when the SCCA revitalized the faltering Can-Am by adopting rules that called for cars that were little more than F-5000 chassis with bodywork.

**FORMULA ATLANTIC**: Tremendously popular class of small engined (1.6 litre), open wheel cars in North America, England, Australia, New Zealand, South Africa and Asia. In the 1970s the North American series was largely run in Canada with some races in the USA, producing some of the greatest talents of the decade, including Gilles Villeneuve, Keke Rosberg, Bobby Rahal and Danny Sullivan. Never supported whole-heartedly by the SCCA, Formula Atlantic suffered a decline in the 1980s but has been revived through the support of Toyota.

**FULL COURSE YELLOW**: When an Indy car race is temporarily slowed to a safe speed and no passing is permitted to enable safety workers to clean-up the scene of an accident or remove debris and fluids from the race track. The situation is signalled when the starter waves a pair of crossed yellow flags and, on ovals, a series of yellow lights around the perimeter of the track are turned on. Full course yellows occur occasionally on road and street circuits.

**GRIP**: In a word, traction.

**GROOVE**: The fastest path(s) around a given turn or, especially on ovals, a race track. Owing to driver styles, different cars and changing conditions, there may be more than one groove on a given track.

**GROUND EFFECTS**: Using the air passing between the car and the race track surface to create downforce which holds the car to the road, increasing its cornering capabilities. First developed in the Lotus 78 F1 car during the 1977 season, ground effects – first applied to Indy car ovals in 1979 with the Chaparral 2K – resulted in enormous increases in lap speeds.

**INDY CAR**: A relatively recent term, now used to describe the cars which compete in the PPG Indy Car World Series national championship. Prior to 1971, however, more than one type of car was required to compete in the national championship series as the schedule included races on dirt ovals. The cars which were used on the paved tracks such as Phoenix, Indianapolis and Milwaukee were called "Champ cars".

**IMS**: The Indianapolis Motor Speedway

**IMSA**: The International Motor Sports Association was originally a spin off of the Sports Car Club of America founded by John Bishop. After initially running sedan and sports cars races, IMSA eventually took over the sports prototype racing in North America with its highly successful Camel GT series. With the demise of sports car racing

worldwide in recent years, however, IMSA has fallen on hard times and its future is uncertain.

**LEAN**: Refers to the air/fuel mixture (see also RICH). Indy car drivers can regulate the fuel mixture from the cockpit and thus adjust the car's performance to their specific circumstances. For example, a driver trying to stretch the distance between fuel stops may "lean-out" the fuel mixture.

**LOOSE**: When the back end of a car has less adhesion – or grip – than the front end, resulting in a tendency for cornering with the rear end "hanging out". Also known as oversteer. In small doses, oversteer can be beneficial on a road course but is almost always undesirable on the high speed ovals.

**LOCAL YELLOW**: When the race is slowed only in the immediate vicinity of an incident; signalled by corner workers waving a yellow flag at the site.

**MARBLES**: Small, loose pieces of rubber and pavement that accumulate on the track during the course of the race, usually just off the line or groove. A driver who strays "onto the marbles" will often loose control because of dramatically reduced traction.

**MIDGETS**: Raced on dirt and paved ovals throughout North America, midgets are front engined, open wheel "formula" cars with a wheel-base limited to six feet. For long the first step on the rung of serious professional racing, these cars were supplanted by Super Vee and Formula Atlantic in the 1970s as the preferred stepping stone for aspiring Indy car drivers. Midgets continued to be a popular racing class in its own right, however, and USAC's Jolly Rancher Series attracts oversubscribed entries wherever it goes.

**NHRA**: The National Hot Rod Association is the leading US sanctioning body for drag racing, where two cars race from a standing start on ¼ mile long "drag strips".

**NASCAR**: The National Association of Stock Car Racing is the leading US sanctioning body for stock (aka saloon) car racing. Its premier series, the Winston Cup, consists of 31 races concentrated in the Southeastern United States but also with races in California, Michigan and New York. NASCAR also sanctions numerous "junior" series such as the Winston West and Busch Grand National series.

**OFF-ROAD RACING**: Form of racing popularized in Southern California but gaining fans throughout the United States, in which cars, trucks, motorcycles and dune buggies race over natural terrain. The most famous off-road race is the Baja 1000, which runs from Ensenada to La Paz, Mexico through the largely trackless Baja California. In recent years, stadium racing – in which courses simulating natural terrain are constructed on the floors of large outdoor stadiums usually reserved for baseball and football games – has become an increasingly popular form of the sport.

**OVERSTEER**: see LOOSE

**PACE CAR**: Before each Indy car race, a modified street car leads the starting field around the track (usually for three laps at moderate speed to allow the cars to warm up). The pace car pulls off shortly before the start of the race. The pace car is also used to "pace" the field during a full course yellow.

**POP-OFF VALVE**: A spring-actuated valve that limits the amount of boost pressure transmitted to the engine by the turbocharger. Once the pressure exceeds its preset limit (in the case of CART's race engines, 45in of mercury absolute), the pop-off valve opens and "de-pressurizes" the intake manifold, causing severe loss of power.

**PPG**: The former Pittsburgh Plate Glass Company changed its name in 1968 to PPG Industries in order to reflect its diversification into automotive and industrial coatings, flat glass and continuous strand fibre glass, chemicals, medical electronics and architectural finishes. PPG began sponsoring the CART Indy car series in 1980 and will contribute some $4.75 million in total prize money to the 1993 series. The 1993 PPG Cup title alone was worth $1 million – and went to Nigel Mansell officially on the day after the final race.

**PUSH**: When the front end of a car has less adhesion – or grip – than the rear end, resulting in a tendency for the front end to "plough" or "push" straight ahead in a corner. Also known as understeer. Most drivers prefer a slight push on the ovals.

**RESTART**: Following a full course yellow, Indy car races are restarted in single file order. Drivers and teams are informed of the impending "restart" by CART officials, by the starter, who holds his index finger in the air at the start of the final lap of the full course yellow and by the pace car, which turns out its flashing lights midway through the final lap of a full course yellow.

**RICH**: Refers to the air/fuel mixture (see *also* LEAN). The richer (more fuel) the mixture, the higher the power output – also the lower the fuel economy.

**SCRUB**: Small and frequent changes in direction by the driver to rough up – or scrub - new tyres or generate heat in worn tyres before the start of a race or during a full course yellow.

**SET-UP**: The combination of suspension settings (camber, castor, toe-in), ride height, damper and spring settings, and wing positioning on a car at any given time. Drivers struggling to turn fast laps are said to be "searching for the set-up."

**SHUNT**: A minor accident that does not involve significant damage to car or driver.

**SILVER CROWN CARS**: Also known as champ dirt cars, this front engined, open wheel "formula" car has a wheel base limited to eight feet and a maximum engine size of

355 cubic inches. Once the staple of the national championship series, these cars now run in the USAC Silver Crown series which is centred in the Midwest but also includes races on the dirt mile at Sacramento, California and the paved oval at Phoenix International Raceway.

**SPRINT CARS**: Open wheel "formula" cars with wheel base limited to seven feet, and a maximum engine size of 410 cubic inches raced on dirt and paved ovals throughout North America. The two main sprint car sanctioning bodies – USAC and the World of Outlaws – differ in their rules regarding aerodynamic devices, as the WoO permits gigantic wings to be a fixed atop the car's roll cage, while USAC prohibits wings. The WoO series is one of the most gruelling calendars in racing; with more than 70 races in 21 states and Mexico between February and November.

**STAGGER**: On the left turn only ovals, teams use a slightly larger diametre tyre on the right rear to help the car turn. The difference is slight, as little as $\frac{1}{10}$in. Increasing or decreasing the amount of stagger during pit stops – by changing to a larger or smaller right rear – is one way in which drivers try to improve their set-up during the race.

**STREET CIRCUIT**: Race track which uses the everyday streets of a city or town, blocked-off for racing purposes by guardrail and cement barriers .

**SUPERSPEEDWAY**: Although there is no firm definition, a superspeedway is an oval, with steeply banked turns and, in contrast to a bullring, is more than mile in length.

**SUPER VEE**: Like Formula Atlantic, Super Vee was a "junior" formula featuring 1.6 litre Volkswagen engines that was popular in

Europe and North America. In North America, the Super Vee series was contested on both road circuits and ovals and became the preferred training ground for Indy cars

from the mid-1970s to the late 1980s. In contrast, Formula Atlantic was seen as the road to Formula One. In that regard, Super Vee was surely the more successful, as every series champion from 1975 to 1989 save one eventually drove Indy cars. The Super Vee series was disbanded in 1990 following financial reversals suffered by Volkswagen's North American operations.

**SCCA**: The Sports Car Club of America is the Colorado-based organization that sanctions amateur road racing, amateur and professional rallying activities in the Unites States, together with selected professional racing series such as the Trans-Am and, in the past, the Can-Am and F5000.

**TRI-OVAL**: An oval with three instead of four turns. On the Indy car schedule, only Nazareth Speedway is a tri-oval. The most famous tri-oval is Daytona International Speedway in Florida.

**UNDERSTEER**: see PUSH.

**UNDERTRAY**: More than just the bottom of the race car, the undertray is a piece of carbon-fibre carefully shaped to manage the flow of air underneath the car to create downforce.

**USAC**: The United States Auto Club sanctioned the national championship from 1956 through 1978 before the advent of CART. Since CART took over the national championship, USAC has continued to sanction the Indianapolis 500 as well as a host of other open wheeled racing classes, ranging from midgets to sprint and champ dirt cars, as well as the Pikes Peak Hillclimb and occasional speed record runs.

**WAKE**: The disturbed or turbulent air left behind a race car.

**WINGS**: The appendages on the front and rear of race cars, they are shaped like inverted airplane wings in order to create downforce rather than lift.

# Indy car: Acknowledgements

**DAVID PHILLIPS** is a freelance journalist whose primary work consists of covering the sport of Indy car racing for *Autoweek* Magazine, one of the leading automotive publications in the USA (weekly circulation 275,000), and *Motoring News* – the UK's oldest car publication. David files race-by-race reports on each of the 16 races in the PPG/Indycar World Series (including the Indianapolis 500) and provides weekly updates on developments in the sport.

David has also been a correspondent for *On Track* magazine, editor-at-large for *Sports Car* magazine, and contributor to *Auto Hebdo* (France), *Racing On* (Japan), *The Independent* (UK) and *USA Today*. He has also been ghosting a regular Nigel Mansell column for *Autoweek*. David is a member of the American Racing Press Association.

**ART FLORES** was born in an Arizona ghost town and has been based in the San Francisco Bay Area since age one. He tried out club car racing at age 20, but switched to racing photography with a ten-year stint covering Formula 1 and Le Mans. He has been covering CART racing virtually fulltime and is series photographer for *Motoring News* (UK). He has covered assignments for *Racing On* (Japan), *Auto y Pista* (Mexico), *Autoweek* (USA), *Road & Track* (USA), *Auto Motor Sport* (Greece), *Automobile* (USA), *Car & Driver* (USA), and *Excellence* (USA). His pictures have appeared in numerous national newspapers and advertisements. He is currently working for two Indy car teams as well as series sponsors and support series teams.

**Bob Tronolone** supplied the historic photographs – pages 9, 16, 18/19, 20/21, 22/23, 24/25, 25/26, 27/28, 30/31. Bob has shot every Indianapolis 500 since 1961 and is based in Burbank, California, where he runs Automobile Racing Photography.

Other picture acknowledgements:
**Allsport**: Indy 500, page 92-93 and Mansell, page 64.
**Daily Mail**: Indy car artwork, page 11.
**Quadrant Picture Library/Autocar**: historic shots pages 16 & 18.
**Dick Parnham**: Budweiser dragster, page 126.

All other pictures by **Art Flores**.

**David Phillips** would also like to thank Gordo and Jeremy for their proofreading help; Steve for hiring him in the first place; DJT, MS and Green Jumper for moral support; and Joseph White, a lover of words.

**Cooling Brown** would also like to thank:
**Barry Bronson** at Valvoline for the use of the cutaway artwork, pages 12-13.
**Tony Matthews,** UK illustrator of this highly detailed artwork, and for his personal help.
**Matthew Hooper** at the Mansell Andretti Information Bureau for race result information.
**Mike McEvoy** at Sports Management Network.
**Dee Beman** at Championship Auto Racing Teams, Inc.; and last but by no means least
**Johnny Harrison** for his non-stop support and encouragement to do this book.

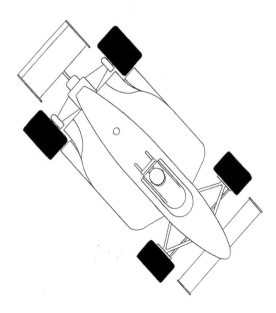

128